G000130935

PLACES
in the BIBLE

ENCOUNTER 125

CITIES, VILLAGES &

'ORDINARY' PLACES

DR. WOODROW KROLL

HOST OF RADIO'S *Back to the Bible*

Nashville, Tennessee

Project Editor: Kathy Baker

Designed by The DesignWorks Group, www.thedesignworksgroup.com

ISBN 1–4041–0174–8

Printed and bound in China

www.thomasnelson.com
www.jcountryman.com

www.backtothebible.org

*"You shall seek the place
where the* LORD *your God chooses . . .
and there you shall go."*

DEUTERONOMY 12:5

Contents

*LORD, I have loved
the habitation of Your house,
And the place where Your glory dwells.*

PSALM 26:8

INTRODUCTION

Everything has to happen somewhere. That's why places are important. Battles make insignificant places—Vicksburg, Corrigidor, Fallujah—forever famous. There are places where we are invigorated by the thrill of victory, and places we are deflated by the agony of defeat. Mention the name of a place and you stir up a memory. Yankee Stadium. Bora Bora. That little café where you first met. Places are the "stick pins" on the map of life.

The Bible is filled with such places, interesting places. Stories can't happen without people and places. If you enjoy getting to know the Bible by getting to know its people better, you'll surely enjoy getting to know its places better too. Bible places are where God often touched the lives of Bible people.

Jacob came back to God at Bethel. Cleopas encountered the resurrected Christ at Emmaus. Abraham left Ur of the Chaldees to become the man of faith. Jonah left Joppa to become the man of fear. And Saul left Tarsus to become the apostle Paul. Places matter.

So from A to Z, get ready to explore 125 of the thousands of hamlets, cities, and "ordinary" places in the Bible. Many will be familiar to you; some will not. But the fact they are recorded in the Bible means they each have a story to tell.

When you read of these places, become a part of that story. Enter into what's happening. Find God there. That's how to make Bible places, your places.

*In His hand
are the deep
places
of the earth*

ADAM

Sometimes You Gotta Get Your Feet Wet

An old proverb says that the journey of a thousand miles begins with a single step. While that's true, taking that first step can be pretty scary.

The Israelites had wandered in the wilderness for forty years. Then they came to a grove of acacia trees

NAME: "Red" or "Ground"
LOCATION: 35 miles NE of Jerusalem, p.33
IDENTIFICATION: Town near Zarethan at junction of Jabbok and Jordan Rivers
STORY LINE: Here Jordan's waters backed up during Israel's crossing
READ IT IN THE BIBLE: Joshua 3:1–17

just east of the Jordan River and were about to enter the Promised Land at last. Joshua told the people, *"Sanctify yourselves, for tomorrow the LORD will do wonders among you"* (Joshua 3:5), and wonders He did.

As the priests edged near the water their faith was challenged. Would they make it across the swollen waters of the Jordan or be swept away in the flood?

They didn't know, but they trusted God and stepped into the water. The waters miraculously backed up all the way to Adam, a village near Zaretan on the eastern bank of the river, near the confluence of the Jabbok and the Jordan (Joshua 3:16). The threat was removed by God. Faith won out over fear. The people followed the priests and walked across the dry river bed to their promised homeland.

Has God been impressing upon you something He wants you to undertake? Perhaps it's to witness to a friend. Maybe it's to launch out in a new ministry. Whatever God is calling you to do, remember that the first step is the hardest. God will roll back your obstacles to success, but first you've got to get your feet wet, like the priests did. Only then will you see Him work in your life. Take the first step; He'll do the rest.

ADRIATIC SEA

Praying in Public

Is prayer a private matter? Sometimes it is, but thankful people pray in public, too. King David vowed to give thanks to God among the nations that surrounded him (Psalm 18:49) and so should we.

When Paul was making his fateful journey to Rome, his ship encountered rough Adriatic seas. The Adriatic

NAME: "Without Wood"
LOCATION: S and E of Italy, p.12
IDENTIFICATION: The gulf between Italy and the coast of Croatia and Greece
STORY LINE: Paul thanked God in public for the food he had to eat
READ IT IN THE BIBLE: Acts 27:1–38

was named after the town of Adria near the mouth of the Po River in Italy. Although it mostly lies between Italy and Greece, the name was extended by New Testament times to include the gulf of the Mediterranean Sea between Crete and Sicily as well. There Paul's ship was tossed about for two weeks, but when all hope of survival was gone, an angel of the Lord assured the apostle no lives would be lost. In order to encourage the other passengers, two hundred seventy–six in all, *"He took bread and gave thanks to God in the presence of them all; and when he had broken it he began to eat"* (Acts 27:35).

If you're reticent to say grace before meals because others might see you, follow the lead of Paul. He didn't hesitate at all to thank God in front of others. Neither did Jesus before He fed the five thousand (Matthew 14:19), or the four thousand (Matthew 15:36). At the Last Supper, *"Jesus took bread, blessed and broke it, and gave it to the disciples"* (Matthew 26:26).

You needn't make a show of your gratitude, but you needn't fear showing it either. *"Surely the righteous shall give thanks to Your name"* (Psalm 140:13). Let your light shine today even as a silent witness before a watching world (Matthew 5:16).

ADULLAM

Be Careful What You Say

During World War II a common expression was, "Loose lips sink ships." It was a meaningful warning that careless conversation, overhead by the enemy, could have disastrous consequences.

David was taking refuge in a limestone cave near the ancient city of Adullam. He often found himself

NAME: "Refuge"
LOCATION: 18 miles S of Jerusalem, p.33
IDENTIFICATION: A Canaanite royal city conquered by Joshua
STORY LINE: The cave of Adullam was David's frequent refuge from danger
READ IT IN THE BIBLE: 2 Samuel 23:8–17

there. It was a refuge when he fled from King Saul (1 Samuel 22:1) and a stronghold in his war against the Philistines (2 Samuel 23:13–17). David wrote Psalms 57 and 142 while holed up in this cave.

Once when Bethlehem was being occupied by Philistine troops, David nostalgically wished for a drink of water from the well at the gate of the village. It was just a simple musing, but three of David's crack commandos overheard him and undertook a dangerous mission. They sneaked off to Bethlehem, fought their way through the Philistine troops to snatch water from the well, and then fought their way back to David. But he was so embarrassed at the danger these three mighty men put themselves in for his sake that, instead of drinking the water, David poured it out as an offering to the Lord.

David's wish was innocent enough, but it reminds us how careful we must be of what we say, especially when we think no one is listening. Perhaps this is when David learned to pray, *"Let the words of my mouth and the meditation of my heart be acceptable in Your sight, O LORD, my strength and my redeemer"* (Psalm 19:14).

Jesus said, *"for every idle word men may speak, they will give account"* (Matthew 12:36). That's reason enough to guard your lips.

AIJALON

Is Anything Too Hard For God?

Have you ever wondered if your need was beyond the reach of God? Did there seem to be no way God could answer your financial, physical, or even spiritual request? Did you pray in faith anyway?

When a coalition of warlords threatened the Gibeonites, the Israelites were obliged to protect their

NAME: "Place of the Deer"
LOCATION: 15 miles NW of Jerusalem, p.33
IDENTIFICATION: A Levitical city overlooking a flat, broad valley
STORY LINE: Joshua directed the sun to stand still in the Valley of Aijalon
READ IT IN THE BIBLE: Joshua 10:1–15

vassal subjects. True military genius that he was, Joshua led Israel's finest soldiers on a forced march from Gilgal eighteen miles in under ten hours. This quick response caught the coalition off guard. When the enemy attempted to escape, God pelted them with a violent hailstorm. More of the enemy died by the pounding hail than by the swords of Israel's soldiers.

But Joshua needed to eliminate this threat completely, so he asked God for the impossible. The words of Joshua 10:12, *"Sun, stand still over Gibeon; And Moon, in the Valley of Aijalon"* are part of his prayer recorded in the Book of Jasher. Would God actually cause the sun to stop or slow its movement in the sky? Theologians have argued over this passage for centuries without much hope of explanation.

But more remarkable than the halting of the sun was the faith of Joshua. The fact Joshua actually believed he could ask God to do something so unprecedented is astounding. Consequently, *"there has been no day like that, before it or after it, that the LORD heeded the voice of a man"* (v. 14).

Is there anything too hard for God? Not if He wills it. So, next time you think your request doesn't stand a chance, pray anyway. Maybe a chance is all it needs.

AKELDAMA

Betrayal

One of the most popular names for boys in the United States recently has been a biblical name—Jacob. But it's no coincidence that parents never use another biblical name—Judas. Since the night he betrayed Jesus, Judas' name has been synonymous with treachery.

NAME: "Place of Blood"
LOCATION: South side of Jerusalem, p.53
IDENTIFICATION: The field bought by the priests after Judas betrayed Jesus
STORY LINE: Judas hanged himself in the Field of Akeldama
READ IT IN THE BIBLE: Matthew 27:3–10; Acts 1:18–20

Judas walked the dusty roads of Galilee with the disciples, but his heart never beat with theirs. He prearranged with Jerusalem's religious leaders to convey Jesus peacefully into their hands and received thirty pieces of silver as payment for his disloyalty. The quiet peace of the Garden of Gethsemane was shattered when Judas invaded it with a *"great multitude"* of angry people (Matthew 26:47). With a simple kiss of feigned friendship the Savior was betrayed. The mob led Him away for trial and crucifixion.

But then a strange thing happened. Judas suffered the pangs of guilt. He returned to the chief priests and elders, threw the silver coins to the floor, and in shame and remorse went out and hanged himself in a field (Matthew 27:3–10). The religious leaders used the money to purchase that field to bury indigent strangers. The site has been identified with the Potter's House (Jeremiah 18:2–12; compare Zechariah 11:13) located just south of Jerusalem in the Valley of Hinnom (Acts 1:19). It was called Akeldama, "field of blood," because it was purchased with tainted blood money.

Betrayal can take many forms. Each day we all must guard our hearts so that we do not betray the Savior in our thoughts, words, or deeds.

AMMON

Most Unlikely to Succeed

Sometimes the most unlikely people turn out to be heroes. One night at Taco Bell, 17–year old Nicholas Zenns was taking orders at the drive–up window when a pregnant woman appeared before him screaming in hard labor. The high–school student pulled off his

NAME: "People"
LOCATION: E of Israel, pp.13 & 33
IDENTIFICATION: Land of the Ammonites, Israel's kin and
   perpetual enemies
STORY LINE: The outcast Jephthah defeated Ammon
READ IT IN THE BIBLE: Judges 11:1–33

headset, called the paramedics, and then delivered the baby. He became an unlikely hero.

Jephthah's heroics against the Ammonites made him an unlikely hero, too. The Ammonites were a powerful people who lived in the fertile area east of the Jordan River, from the Arnon and Jabbok Rivers eastward to the Syrian Desert. They traced their ancestry to the younger daughter of Lot (Genesis 19:38), making the Ammonites and the Israelites distant relatives, but enemies nevertheless. The main Ammonite city was Rabbah, today Amman, the capital of Jordan.

At the end of the twelfth century B.C. the Ammonites attacked the Israelites living in Gilead and then crossed the Jordan and attacked the tribes of Judah, Benjamin, and Ephraim (Judges 10:7–9). In desperation the elders of Gilead turned for help to Jephthah, who was a social outcast but an able military leader (11:1–11). He defeated the Ammonites so decisively that it was unnecessary for him to wage further campaigns against Ammonite settlements west of the Jordan (11:12–33).

If you suffer from the "least likely syndrome," take a page from Jephthah's journal. It's not where you come from that's important; it's where you're going. Trust God and be open to every possibility.

ANTIOCH

Just Call Me 'Christian'

Being a Christian has never been easy.

Antioch was the capital of Syria and an important city in the Roman Empire. Situated on the banks of the Orontes River, about fifteen miles from where the river empties into the Mediterranean, Antioch was built

NAME: "Driven Against"
LOCATION: N of Israel, p.13
IDENTIFICATION: Capital of Syria and the third largest city of the Roman Empire
STORY LINE: Followers of Jesus were first called "Christians" at Antioch
READ IT IN THE BIBLE: Acts 11:19–26

around 300 B.C. In ancient times the city's population numbered half a million. Antioch was a busy commercial, religious, intellectual, and political center.

But Antioch played an important role in the formation of Christianity as well. Followers of Jesus fled to Antioch to escape fierce persecution in Jerusalem (Acts 11:19). Paul and Barnabas taught the Word to the fledgling church there. A crucial meeting to decide if Gentiles could become part of God's family was held there (Acts 15). Antioch was the church from which Christian missionaries were first sent out to win the world to Christ. But most notably, believers in Jesus Christ were first tagged "Christians" by the people of Antioch (11:26). It's a name that stuck.

Being a Christian in the 21st century is becoming increasingly like being a Christian in the first century. Respected for centuries, Christians today are increasingly denied good-paying jobs, harassed and persecuted for their faith, and even targeted for death by extremists. If you haven't prayed for the persecuted church recently, take some time today to do so. Pray for their protection, their provision, and their boldness. You may not feel the sting of persecution yourself, but when one Christ-follower hurts, the whole Body hurts.

ANTIOCH IN PISIDIA

Shake Off the Dust

Does it seem like sometimes your witness for the Lord is falling on deaf ears? Paul and Barnabas knew the feeling.

On their first missionary journey they docked at Perga on the south coast of modern Turkey and made their way inland to Antioch in Pisidia. This city was so

NAME: "Driven Against" and "Pitchy"
LOCATION: Central Turkey, p.13
IDENTIFICATION: City in Phrygia, capital of the Roman province of Galatia
STORY LINE: Paul was harassed for his preaching and forced to leave
READ IT IN THE BIBLE: Acts 13:14–32, 42–52

named to distinguish it from other cities of the same name. Pisidian Antioch was a commercial center and in A.D. 25 became capital of the Roman province of Galatia (Acts 13:14–52).

When Paul and Barnabas arrived they went into the synagogue on the Sabbath and quietly took a seat. But because Paul was a trained rabbi, the rulers of the synagogue invited him to speak. The Jews didn't seem much impressed, but after the service ended the Gentile on–lookers begged Paul to return the next Sabbath. He did and shocked the worshippers by saying that because Israel had turned a deaf ear toward God, Jehovah had turned His saving grace toward the Gentiles. Unheard of! Unthinkable! But true.

The enthusiastic Gentile crowds that gathered to hear Paul threatened the tranquility of the town. As a result the Jewish leaders incited men and women to hassle Paul and Barnabas and expel them from the area.

If you have ever felt your witness for Christ was ineffective, remember Antioch in Pisidia. There Paul and Barnabas simply shook the dust off their sandals and moved on to neighboring Iconium. Sometimes you have to do the same. When your witness is unappreciated, don't think you've failed. You've simply identified your Pisidian Antioch. There are more fertile fields ahead. Perhaps God wants you to move on to them.

ARABIA

Time to Get Away

Do you need a little time to yourself? Some "me" time? Many of us think we do.

After Paul's dramatic conversion on the road to Damascus he had much to learn. He knew the Torah, but little of God and His grace. He needed a place to

NAME: "Desert"
LOCATION: S of Israel, p.13 & 33
IDENTIFICATION: Peninsula bounded by Red Sea, Indian Ocean, and Persian Gulf
STORY LINE: Multiple Bedouin tribes from Arabia interacted with Israel
READ IT IN THE BIBLE: Galatians 1:11–18

get away where God could reveal Himself to Paul. That place was Arabia.

Just over a million square miles, about one–third the area of the United States, Arabia was a large peninsula bounded on the west by the Red Sea, on the south by the Indian Ocean and on the east by the Persian Gulf. It is an arid, inhospitable land that was populated only by nomadic tribes—the perfect place for Paul to get away.

Galatians 1:17 places Paul's Arabian getaway during his years in Damascus. After his conversion, Paul did not go up to Jerusalem to confer with the other apostles. Instead, he left Damascus, huddled with God in Arabia, returned to Damascus, and three years later visited the Jerusalem apostles. The Bible does not say that Paul spent all three years in Arabia (see vv. 17–18), but his retreat into the wilderness gave him the needed time alone with God to prepare for a great work.

Are you in need of some time alone with God? Do you need His direction for a big decision in your life? Perhaps you don't need "me" time at all. What you need is "God" time. That's how you discover His will and His way for your life, as Paul did. Make that time in your schedule today, and God will give you clear direction for tomorrow.

"As a shepherd seeks out his flock on the day he is among his scattered sheep, so will I seek out My sheep and deliver them from all the places where they were scattered on a cloudy and dark day."

EZEKIEL 34:12

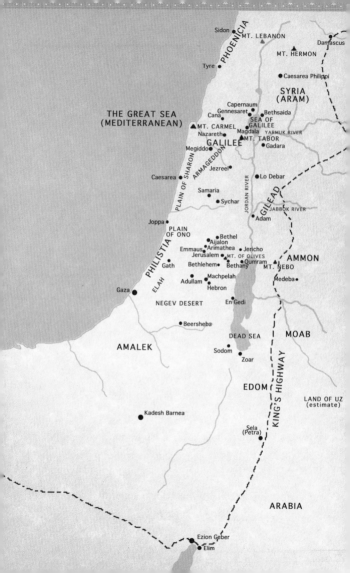

ARARAT

Faith Makes the Difference

Interviewer Larry King was quoted as saying, "I can't make that leap that a lot of people around me have made into belief that there's some judge somewhere." A lot of people are that way. Maybe you are.

NAME: "The Curse Reversed"

LOCATION: Eastern Turkey, Armenia, p.13

IDENTIFICATION: Rugged mountain range in Armenia, just south of the Black Sea

STORY LINE: Noah's ark came to rest on the mountains of Ararat

READ IT IN THE BIBLE: Genesis 8:1–22

In the days of Noah, *"The LORD saw that the wickedness of man was great in the earth, and that every intent of the thoughts of his heart was only evil continually"* (Genesis 6:5). With a worldwide flood, God both judged sin and demonstrated grace. Noah and his family were saved because God told them in advance to build an ark and ride out the year–long disaster.

When the flood waters finally receded, Noah's ark settled on Ararat, a steep, rugged range of mountains just south of the Black Sea. The mountain range covers extreme eastern Turkey, southern Georgia, and northern Iran.

Many expeditions have climbed Mount Ararat in an attempt to locate Noah's ark. Much of this effort has been concentrated around a 17,000 foot peak called Agri Dagh, which is Turkish for "Mountain of Trouble." Local tribesmen call this peak Kohl Nu, "Mount of Noah." And while each expedition has fueled speculation, all of them have failed to find the ark.

Would it make any difference if the ark was located? Not to those who choose not to believe. Finding the ark may confirm your faith in the biblical record, but facts don't produce faith. *"Faith is . . . the evidence of things not seen"* (Hebrews 11:1). If you're having trouble believing the Bible, pray for God to increase your faith. It's faith that makes the difference.

AREOPAGUS

You'll Always Have the Philosophers

On his second missionary journey, Paul and friends came to the city of Philippi. Here Silas and he were jailed for preaching the Gospel (Acts 16:23). When released, they made their way to Thessalonica and were driven out of there, too. During the night they fled to

NAME: "The Hill of Ares"
LOCATION: Near Acropolis in Athens, p.12 (Athens)
IDENTIFICATION: Rocky hill NW of the Acropolis overlooking Athens' agora
STORY LINE: Paul debated the Greek philosophers about the resurrection
READ IT IN THE BIBLE: Acts 17:16–34

Berea, and eventually Paul was forced to travel south to Athens, leaving Silas, Timothy, and Luke in Thessalonica (Acts 17:10–15).

Now the apostle was all alone. It was time to kick back a bit. Sit around the pool. Nurse his wounds. Get some much deserved "R and R." But when Paul saw statues of gods all over the city, his inner spirit was agitated. Petronius, a writer at Nero's court, said satirically that it was easier to find a god in Athens than to find a man. Paul spoke out against this polytheism, first in the synagogue and then in the marketplace.

That's when the Epicureans and Stoics confronted him. They wanted to argue. They took Paul to the Areopagus, a bald, rocky hill northwest of the Acropolis. Popularly known as Mars Hill, five centuries earlier this site was where Socrates had faced those who accused him of making comments against the Greek gods. But this time it was a philosophical discussion of the resurrection of the dead that drew philosophers from all over the city.

If you have witnessed to your friends, you've probably encountered the "philosophers" too. They want to argue about everything. But Paul refused to enter into debate. Instead, using language they would understand, he simply told the God story. You should do the same. You'll always have the philosophers. Make sure they always have the truth.

ARIMATHEA

Destined to Win

Dave trusted Christ as a teenager, but his faith flew under the radar of his friends. No one knew he was a Christian. When he enrolled in college, however, Dave had a "deciding moment" one day in a science class. The professor was ridiculing God and the

NAME: "A Height"
LOCATION: 8 miles NW of Jerusalem, p.33
IDENTIFICATION: Hometown of Joseph, member of the Jerusalem Sanhedrin
STORY LINE: Joseph buried Jesus' body in his Jerusalem family tomb
READ IT IN THE BIBLE: Mark 15:33–47

Christian faith, something that's permissible in most universities. Dave knew he had to do something. He stood up and challenged the professor. Dave's years of being a secret disciple suddenly evaporated. Amazingly, when he sat down, the class broke into applause.

Dave had much in common with Joseph of Arimathea. Although its exact location is unknown, many identify Arimathea with the small village known as Ramathaim–zophim, the hometown of the prophet Samuel, about eight miles northwest of Jerusalem. Joseph was a member of the Sanhedrin, the supreme Jewish council in the days of Jesus (Luke 23:50). The Sanhedrin had seventy–one members divided into three categories: high priests, elders, and scribes. Joseph was probably an elder, a wealthy and distinguished layman (Mark 15:43).

Joseph had become a secret follower of the Lord Jesus, but when Christ was crucified, Joseph had his own "deciding moment." Risking everything, he went to Pilate and asked permission to bury the body of Jesus. Nearby was Joseph's family tomb, and Jesus was the first person to use it.

The crucifixion changed everything for Joseph, just like the classroom did for Dave. If you're struggling to be public about your faith, pray that when your "deciding moment" comes, God will give you the courage to do what Dave and Joseph of Arimathea did. You'll never be the same.

ARMAGEDDON

Is Anything Too Hard For God?

Have you noticed that often a place is identified by a single event? Hiroshima. My Lai. Columbine. That's also true of Armageddon.

The word "Armageddon" actually refers to the mound on which the town of Megiddo was built and

NAME: "Mountain of Megiddo"
LOCATION: 55 miles N. of Jerusalem, pp.13 & 33
IDENTIFICATION: Valley in southern Galilee between Megiddo and the Jordan Valley
STORY LINE: Scene of the apocalyptic battle between Christ and Antichrist
READ IT IN THE BIBLE: Revelation 16:1–16

the valley that lies before it. Megiddo was strategically located in northern Israel between the sands of the Mediterranean and the broad plain of Jezreel. It has been the scene of many important battles in Israel's history. Sisera was routed by the armies of Deborah and Barak there (Judges 4–5). Gideon defeated the Midianites and Amalekites there (Judges 6–7). King Saul and his army were defeated by the Philistines in this valley (1 Samuel 31). And there King Josiah was slain in battle by the Egyptian army of Pharaoh Necho (2 Kings 23:29). Britain's General Allenby, who fought there in World War I, claimed that the valley of Megiddo was the most perfect battleground in the world.

Chapters 15 and 16 of Revelation describe seven angels pouring out seven bowls of God's wrath upon the earth. The sixth angel pours out his bowl upon the great river Euphrates. Its waters dry up, preparing the way for the march of the "kings from the east" on Israel. Three demonic spirits prompt the kings of the world to gather for a catastrophic confrontation between good and evil on these wind-swept plains.

The outcome of the battle is not in doubt. *"The kingdoms of this world have become the kingdoms of our Lord and of His Christ, and He shall reign forever and ever!"* (Revelation 11:15). Take a moment today to thank God that although the present may look grim, the future looks much brighter.

ASSYRIA

The Power of Prayer

Hezekiah was in trouble and he knew it. Sennacherib, king of Assyria, had surrounded Jerusalem and was threatening to attack. This was no idle threat; Assyria had the power to destroy Israel.

Name: "Level Plain"
Location: NE of Israel, p.13
Identification: Powerful kingdom of Mesopotamia; Israel's perpetual nemesis
Story Line: Assyrian armies were defeated by prayer, not weapons
Read it in the Bible: 2 Kings 18:13–19:19

An ancient and powerful kingdom of Mesopotamia, Assyria was located north of Babylonia, in the region of the upper Tigris and Euphrates rivers. It was bounded on the west by the Syrian desert and on the north and east by the Armenian and Persian mountains. And in 701 B.C., Sennacherib was knocking at the door of Jerusalem.

When Hezekiah received a threatening message

from the Assyrian king, he did what came naturally to him. He read it, went quickly to the temple, and turned it over to God (2 Kings 19:14). Then Hezekiah prayed like he had never prayed before. His prayer features all the elements of a prayer that gets hold of God—worship, information, supplication, and more (2 Kings 19:14–19).

When the Jews of Jerusalem got up the next morning it was strangely quiet. No chatter among the Assyrian troops outside the wall. No battle cries. Nothing but the eerie silence of death. God had sent the angel of the Lord into the Assyrian camp during the night, and 185,000 lay dead that morning. Jerusalem was spared because her king knew how to pray.

When you are faced with the most demanding challenges of your life, do you know how to get hold of God? Hezekiah did because he had developed the habit of taking everything to God in prayer. Acquire that same habit and you won't be caught unprepared when you need to pray like you've never prayed before.

ATHENS

Blameless is Better than Sophisticated

Today a popular tourist destination and home to the 2004 Olympics, Athens was once the intellectual center of the world. The city began its rise to glory in the sixth century B.C., first under the leadership of Solon (about 559 B.C.), who established democratic forms of

NAME: "City of Athena"
LOCATION: Southern Greece, p.12
IDENTIFICATION: Principal city of Attica, powerful kingdom in southern Greece
STORY LINE: Paul prays that the Thessalonians will be blameless
READ IT IN THE BIBLE: 1 Thessalonians 3:1–13; Acts 17:1–16

government, and later under Pericles (about 429 B.C.), when the magnificent buildings of the Acropolis were erected. In its golden age, Athens became the center of philosophy, art, architecture, and drama. By the time the apostle Paul visited Athens on his second missionary journey (A.D. 50–53), the city's glory had declined, but its influence continued as Romans spread the city's culture throughout the known world.

But while Paul's body was in esteemed Athens, his heart was in Thessalonica, hundreds of miles to the north. Paul had been forced out of Thessalonica and went to Berea, and soon he made his way to Athens (Acts 17:1–16). He left Silas and Timothy behind to continue the work. Eventually they joined Paul in Athens (1 Thessalonians 3:1–2), but Paul sent Timothy back to Thessalonica to see how the fledgling church was getting along. He was concerned for his fellow believers to be blameless before God (1 Thessalonians 3:13). When Timothy finally caught up with Paul and brought news from Thessalonica (Acts 18:1–5), it gave the apostle an opportunity to write a letter to the Thessalonians about blamelessness.

To be blameless is not the same as to be sinless; God knows you cannot be sinless, but He wants you to be blameless. Blameless means you have nothing to hide. There are no skeletons in your closet. The Athenians were concerned about intellectual minds; God is concerned about pure hearts. He told Abraham, *"Walk before Me and be blameless"* (Genesis 17:1). That's what Paul wanted for the Thessalonians (1 Thessalonians 3:13). That's what He wants for you, too.

BABYLON

Taking a Stand for God

Being faithful to God is most difficult when you face life's greatest challenges. Nobody knew that better than Daniel and his three friends, Hananiah, Mishael, and Azariah.

NAME: "Gate of God"
LOCATION: E of Israel, p.13
IDENTIFICATION: Capital of the Empire between the Tigris and Euphrates Rivers
STORY LINE: Daniel and friends remain true to God during severe difficulty
READ IT IN THE BIBLE: Daniel 1:1–20; 2 Chronicles 36:1–21

In the third year of Judah's King Jehoiakim, Nebuchadnezzar came to power in Babylon. In 605 B.C. the Babylonian king sacked Jerusalem, carrying off the brightest and best of the Jewish teenagers to his palace in Shinar, an ancient name for Babylon (Isaiah 11:11; Zechariah 5:11). Daniel and his three friends were among them.

There they were offered the best of everything to eat,

but these Jewish teenagers chose not to eat the king's delicacies as a matter of principle (Daniel 1:8). For ten days the four teens drank only water and ate only local vegetables. Yet *"at the end of ten days their features appeared better"* than any of the teens who chose to blend into Babylonian society (v. 15).

Standing up for what they believed improved these four physically. It also improved them intellectually because *"God gave them knowledge and skill in all literature and wisdom"* (v. 17). Daniel especially was blessed spiritually for he *"had understanding in all visions and dreams"* (v. 17). They all were better off socially for they found themselves in responsible positions in the king's service before the others did (v. 19).

Does it pay to do the right thing? Ask these teenagers. God has the power not only to preserve but to promote those who take a stand for Him. In the rush for tolerance in our world today, that's something for us to remember as well.

BEERSHEBA

Shattered by Jealousy

On January 6, 1994, the world of figure skating was shocked when one of America's top figure skaters, Nancy Kerrigan, was attacked as she left a practice session at the Olympic trials. What became even more unsettling was when the news broke that the attack

NAME: "Well of Seven"
LOCATION: 53 miles S of Jerusalem, p.33
IDENTIFICATION: Southernmost city of the Promised Land, patriarchal hangout
STORY LINE: Hagar wandered into this area when expelled by Sarah
READ IT IN THE BIBLE: Genesis 21:1–34

may have been motivated by the jealousy of another U.S. figure skater, Tonya Harding.

Jealousy is to the soul what sickness is to the body. It eats away at the core of our being and causes us to do unreasonable, unloving things. It was jealousy that ruined Sarah and almost killed Hagar.

Twenty–eight miles southwest of Hebron was

Beersheba. Abraham gave the city its name when he sent seven ewe lambs to Abimelech as testimony that he had dug a well there (Genesis 21:25–31).

Beersheba also was the site of Sarah's great lapse into jealousy. When Sarah's handmaid, Hagar, gave Abraham a son, bad blood resulted between the two women. Hagar despised Sarah (Genesis 16:4–5) and Sarah treated Hagar harshly (Genesis 16:6). Finally, in a jealous rage, Sarah convinced Abraham that his tent wasn't big enough for both "the other woman" and her, so Hagar and Ishmael were abandoned to the wilderness beyond Beersheba (Genesis 21). Hagar never returned.

If jealousy is eating away at you, see it as the emotional equivalent of acid reflux. It destroys you, not the person of whom you are jealous. God took care of Hagar and Ishmael, but Sarah is forever remembered for her jealous and shameful treatment of them. Jealousy spoils more than your reputation; it ruins your life. Ask God to remove it from you today.

BEREA

Avoiding Bible Illiteracy

Pollster George Gallup Jr. observed, "Americans revere the Bible—but, by and large, they don't read it. And because they don't read it, they have become a nation of biblical illiterates."

NAME: "Well Watered"
LOCATION: 45 miles W of Thessalonica, p.12
IDENTIFICATION: City to which Paul fled from Thessalonian persecution
STORY LINE: Paul commended the Bereans for their study habits
READ IT IN THE BIBLE: Acts 17:1–16

The Church has never been larger, richer, or more ignorant of the Word of God than it is today. I have often said that if Christians blew the dust off their Bibles at the same time, we'd all be killed in the dust storm.

Bible illiteracy was not a problem years ago in a tiny town in Macedonia. Founded in the fifth century B.C., Berea was about twenty–five miles inland from the Aegean Sea in northern Greece. Conquered by Rome in

168 B.C., Berea was one of the most populous Macedonian cities in the time of Christ. Today it is known as Veria.

Paul visited Berea on his second missionary journey (Acts 17:10–15). His companion in ministry, Sopater, lived there (Acts 20:4). When Paul had to flee from religious and political opposition in Thessalonica, Paul and Silas made their way southwest on the highway to Berea. How different their reception was there! Jews and Greeks both eagerly received the Gospel. In fact, Paul was so impressed with their voracious appetite to know God and His Word, he commended the Bereans by saying they *"searched the Scriptures daily"* (Acts 17:11) to discern whether what he taught was true.

A person who merely samples the Bible never acquires much of a taste for it. Don't let a day go by in which you fail to search the Scriptures for guidance, comfort, hope, and more. Be a Berean Christian.

JERUSALEM'S WALLS have been built and destroyed many times through the millenia. Every rebuilding includes some different lines and gates. Here, four major walls are shown together. Some parts of the walls are speculation, and many places overlap through the ages.

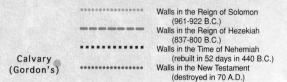

Walls in the Reign of Solomon
(961-922 B.C.)

Walls in the Reign of Hezekiah
(837-800 B.C.)

Walls in the Time of Nehemiah
(rebuilt in 52 days in 440 B.C.)

Walls in the New Testament
(destroyed in 70 A.D.)

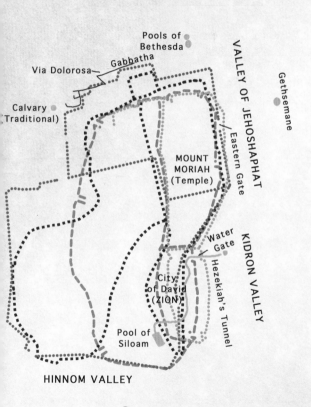

Calvary
(Gordon's)

Pools of
Bethesda

VALLEY OF JEHOSHAPHAT

Via Dolorosa — Gabbatha

Gethsemane

Calvary
(Traditional)

MOUNT OF OLIVES

Eastern Gate

MOUNT
MORIAH
(Temple)

Water
Gate

KIDRON VALLEY

City
of David
(ZION)

Hezekiah's Tunnel

Pool of
Siloam

HINNOM VALLEY

Akeldama

BETHANY

When God Lingers

It seems that every time I'm in a hurry, God isn't. Have you found that to be true? We have both high expectations for God and a timetable for Him to perform them. When He doesn't keep to our schedule, we assume He has let us down.

Name: "House of Unripe Figs"
Location: 2 miles NE of Jerusalem, p.33
Identification: Jerusalem bedroom community on Mount of Olives
Story Line: Jesus raised Lazarus from the dead in Bethany
Read it in the Bible: John 11:1–44

Mary and Martha knew the feeling. They lived in Bethany along with their brother Lazarus. Bethany was on the eastern slope of the Mount of Olives. The family members were good friends with Jesus, so the Savior and His disciples often overnighted there when they were in the Holy City.

But tragedy came suddenly. Lazarus fell ill and died.

Word of Lazarus's illness had been sent immediately to Jesus on the other side of the Jordan River, and the sisters assumed Jesus would hurriedly ascend the Judean hills to Bethany and heal their brother. Instead, Jesus stayed right where He was for two additional days.

In our minds, it is incomprehensible that Jesus would wait so long before helping Lazarus. Jesus knew Lazarus would die, but He also knew that when He raised His friend from the dead, God would receive even greater glory. Jesus was in no hurry because He knew how the story would end.

Mary and Martha couldn't understand Jesus' delay any more than you can understand when you pray and God doesn't seem to answer your prayers. When God lingers, we fret, but we must adapt our expectations to the timetable of Him who makes everything beautiful in its time (Ecclesiastes 3:11). Remember, the One who is never in a hurry is also never late. God's lingering isn't indifference; it's just getting the timing right.

BETHEL

Run Out of Town

A page from John Wesley's diary reads: "Sunday morning, May 5, preached at St. Ann's; was asked not to come back anymore. Sunday p.m., May 5, preached at St. John's; deacons said, 'Get out and stay out.'"

NAME: "House of God"
LOCATION: 11 miles N of Jerusalem, p.33
IDENTIFICATION: Important town on the North–South ridge road of Samaria
STORY LINE: Amos prophesied in Bethel and was run out of town
READ IT IN THE BIBLE: Amos 7:1–17

Wesley wasn't the first preacher to be run out of town. Amos the prophet had the same experience at Bethel.

A Hebrew prophet of the eighth century B.C., Amos hailed from the village of Tekoa, ten miles south of Jerusalem. But he preached in Bethel, eleven miles north of Jerusalem and just over the border from Benjamin in Ephraim's territory. Originally named Luz, the patriarch Jacob changed the name to Bethel meaning "the house of El (God)" (Genesis 28).

When the kingdom divided, in order to keep his people from traveling to Jerusalem to sacrifice, Israel's King Jeroboam I made Bethel one of his royal religious sanctuaries. Here Amos prophesied that Israel would be overrun and the king would be killed. When Amaziah, the priest of Bethel, heard the prophecy of Amos, he accused him of being a traitor and ran him out of town, telling him to go back to Judah and prophesy to his own people. Amos replied, *"I was no prophet, nor was I the son of a prophet. But I was a sheepbreeder . . . and the LORD said to me, 'Go, prophesy to My people, Israel'"* (Amos 7:14–15).

If you feel your witness for the Lord is unappreciated, you're in good company. But be kind. Be truthful. Be compassionate. Be faithful. But don't quit, because God seeks from you what He looked for in Amos and John Wesley—obedience, not acceptance.

BETHESDA

Faith or Superstition

Bethesda is an Aramaic word transliterated into Greek. It was the name of the pool in Jesus' day located just inside the Sheep Gate near the northeastern corner of the Old City of Jerusalem. The pool of Bethesda was

NAME: "House of Grace"
LOCATION: In NE Jerusalem, p.53
IDENTIFICATION: A pool near the Sheep Gate believed to be a "healing zone"
STORY LINE: Jesus healed an infirm man and stirred up a hornet's nest
READ IT IN THE BIBLE: John 5:1–18

surrounded by five porches, or colonnades, that created something of an arcade or promenade around the pool.

When the Franciscan Fathers of the Church of Saint Anne near St. Stephen's Gate began to excavate the site, they found intact two large pools with arched pillars buried under twenty–five to thirty feet of debris. This corresponds to the biblical description of the pool.

One day Jesus encountered a man lying among the

blind, lame, and paralyzed who had positioned themselves near Bethesda. There was an ancient belief that anyone with a disability could be healed if they were the first one into the pool after an angel stirred the waters. Interestingly enough, the last half of verse 3 and all of verse 4 are absent from the earliest Greek manuscripts. We have no evidence of any angelic involvement in healing these people.

Still, when the Lord happened upon the man and asked him if he wanted to be healed, Jesus proved He was more powerful than any superstition. Faith in the Lord Jesus is always well founded. Faith in stories, legends, superstitions, and unexplained phenomena is not.

If you are in need of His divine touch today, ask Jesus to heal you. It may not be His will to do so—He didn't heal every disabled person He encountered—but faith in the certainty of God is superior to faith in anything else.

"Have faith in God" (Mark 11:22).

BETHLEHEM

O Little Town of Bethlehem

It's not much to look at. Called the "City of David" and sometimes Ephrath (Genesis 35:19) to keep it from being confused with another town of the same name in Zebulun's territory, Bethlehem was the home of Boaz, Ruth, Obed, and Jesse (Ruth 4:11–17; 1 Samuel 16:18).

NAME: "House of Bread"
LOCATION: 5 miles S of Jerusalem, p.33
IDENTIFICATION: The "City of David" and his descendants, including the Messiah
STORY LINE: Jesus was born in this tiny village according to divine plan
READ IT IN THE BIBLE: Luke 2:1–20

It was the birthplace of David (1 Samuel 17:12), the shepherd boy who became king.

Today Bethlehem is administered by the Palestinian Authority. Many Christians have been forced out of the city because they are caught in the middle of the Palestinian–Israeli conflict. Still, thousands of pilgrims brave the conflict each year to visit this troubled city.

They come because, as Micah prophesied, *"But you, Bethlehem Ephrathah, though you are little among the thousands of Judah, yet out of you shall come forth to Me the One to be ruler in Israel, whose goings forth are from of old, from everlasting"* (Micah 5:2). Bethlehem is the birthplace of Jesus.

Phillips Brooks showed remarkable insight when in his Christmas hymn "O Little Town of Bethlehem" he wrote:

> *O little town of Bethlehem, how still we see thee lie!*
> *Above thy deep and dreamless sleep the silent stars go by.*
> *Yet in thy dark streets shineth the everlasting light;*
> *The hopes and fears of all the years are met in thee tonight.*

Bring all your hopes and all your fears to the One who conquers fear and releases hope—the Babe of Bethlehem's stable, the Man born to be king. This world may have many religions, but it still has only one Savior. His name is Jesus and He was born in Bethlehem.

BETHSAIDA

The Link of Witness

In 1858 a Sunday school teacher led Dwight L. Moody to the Lord. Moody's evangelistic zeal sparked the heart of F. B. Meyer, who was instrumental in bringing J. Wilbur Chapman to the Lord. Chapman employed Billy Sunday to do evangelistic work, and as a result of

NAME: "House of Fishing"
LOCATION: North side of Sea of Galilee, p.33
IDENTIFICATION: Fishing village, home of Peter, Andrew, James, John, and Philip
STORY LINE: Philip finds the Messiah and quickly finds a friend to tell
READ IT IN THE BIBLE: John 1:43–51

one of Sunday's revivals in Charlotte, North Carolina, a follow–up revival was planned with evangelist Mordecai Hamm. During Hamm's revival, a young man named Billy Graham heard the Gospel and trusted Christ. And so goes the link of witness.

Bethsaida was a fishing village on the north coast of the Sea of Galilee. It was enlarged by Philip the tetrarch

(4 B.C.–A.D. 34), son of Herod the Great, after the death of Caesar Augustus. According to Josephus, Philip the tetrarch later was buried there.

It was at Bethsaida that a blind man was healed (Mark 8:22–26), and nearby Jesus fed more than five thousand people with just five loaves and two fish (Mark 6:34–45). When a resident of Bethsaida named Philip was called to faith and discipleship by the Lord Jesus, he immediately went to his friend Nathanael and said, *"We have found Him of whom Moses in the law, and also the prophets wrote—Jesus of Nazareth"* (John 1:45). When Nathanael questioned whether anything good could come out of a backwater town like Nazareth, Philip simply responded, *"Come and see."* So Nathanael came, saw, and believed in Jesus.

Don't be afraid to be a witness. Sharing the Gospel is simply telling others what Jesus has done for you and inviting them to come see for themselves. You never know what God will do with that person you touch in the link of witness. People need the Lord. Don't be the missing link.

CAESAREA

Exercising Your Rights as a Citizen

Picture this. Soft ocean breezes. Moderate climate. A getaway from the trouble constantly fomenting in Jerusalem. That was Caesarea.

Named in honor of Augustus Caesar, Herod the Great made this seaport city his capital. The 8,000–acre

NAME: "Pertaining to Caesar"
LOCATION: Israel's Mediterranean coast, pp.13 & 33
IDENTIFICATION: Caesarea Maritima was the major seaport for Judah
STORY LINE: Paul appeals to Porcius Festus to honor his Roman civil rights
READ IT IN THE BIBLE: Acts 24:27–25:12

site lies in the plain of Sharon on Israel's Mediterranean coast. Officially known as Caesarea Maritima, three Roman governors administered the country from this chief administrative center: Felix (Acts 24), Festus (Acts 25:1, 4, 6, 13), and Pontius Pilate, whose name was found carved in stone in the theater at Caesarea.

Caesarea is prominent in the New Testament.

The Roman officer Cornelius was converted to Christianity there (Acts 10:1–33). Peter visited Philip, a prominent Christian who lived there (Acts 21:8). Paul spent two years in prison there (Acts 24:27–25:12). As governor, Festus had been in charge only three days when he met with the high priest and chief elders in Jerusalem. They wanted to ambush Paul, but Festus made them come to Caesarea to accuse him in a court of law. When Paul was charged, Festus asked if he would be willing to go to Jerusalem to stand trial, and the apostle replied, *"I stand at Caesar's judgment seat . . . I appeal to Caesar"* (Acts 25:10–11).

Like Paul, who exercised his rights as a Roman citizen, you should not hesitate to exercise your rights as a citizen. God has ordained government for your good (Romans 13:3). Christians need to engage in the civil process, whether it's casting a vote or using the law for protection. Remember to pray for those who govern, but do not hesitate to exercise your rights as a citizen under those for whom you pray.

CAESAREA PHILIPPI

Who Do You Say Jesus Is?

Did you know there's a difference between Caesarea, Philippi, and Caesarea Philippi? Caesarea was the Roman administrative city on Israel's Mediterranean coast. Philippi was a Roman colony in northern Greece. And Caesarea Philippi was a city in northern Israel on

NAME: "Pertaining to Caesar Phillip"
LOCATION: 105 miles N of Jerusalem, p.33
IDENTIFICATION: Caesarea Philippi lies on one of three sources of the Jordan
STORY LINE: Peter confessed, "You are the Christ, the Son of the living God"
READ IT IN THE BIBLE: Matthew 16:13–28

the southern slopes of Mount Hermon. There Wadi Banias, one of the three sources of the Jordan River, springs out of the rock.

Called Panion in the second century B.C. because the Greek god Pan was worshiped there, Josephus (*War* 2.9.1) records that when Herod the Great died, his son "Philip built the city Caesarea, at the fountains of Jordan, and in the region of Paneas." Philip made it his capital and named it Caesarea Philippi after the Roman emperor Tiberius Caesar and himself.

Caesarea Philippi is a great place for some "R and R" and that's what Jesus and His disciples were doing when the Master asked His disciples who people said that He was. After they reported a variety of answers, Jesus asked an even more pointed question: *"Who do you say that I am?"* (Matthew 16:15). Peter's answer was the quintessential Christian confession: *"You are the Christ, the Son of the living God."*

If Jesus asked you that same question, what would your answer be? Is He just a religious leader, an ethical teacher to you? Or is He Messiah, Son of God, Savior? To follow Jesus as a good teacher may make you a better person, but if you want to go to heaven when you die, you must see Him as more. Make sure you know Jesus as your Savior (John 3:14–18; Acts 16:30–31).

CALVARY

Forever Changed

Aren't you amazed at how a single event can forever change our perception of a word? One day changed Columbine from the name of a high school into a killing field. And remember when 9/11 was just an emergency number?

Name: "Skull"
Location: Outside Damascus Gate, p.53
Identification: A place of crucifixion in Jerusalem, called Golgotha in Hebrew
Story Line: Here Jesus died to pay the penalty for mankind's sin
Read it in the Bible: Luke 23:26–49; John 19:1–24

Calvary is the Latin word (used in Luke 23:33) for Golgotha, a place near Jerusalem where executions were carried out by the Roman soldiers. *Golgotha* means "the skull" in Hebrew. The church father Jerome (A.D. 346–420) speculated that the place got its name from the skulls of many crucified victims that were left lying around there. Others have said that this place of the crucifixion was a hill shaped like a skull. Nobody knows for sure. In 1842, Otto Thenius suggested that Calvary was a rocky hill 250 yards northeast of the Damascus Gate. When General Charles Gordon later agreed it became known as "Gordon's Calvary."

The important thing is not where Calvary is but what happened there. One day this horrible, ugly place of death was transformed into a place of beauty and hope because Jesus Christ died there for our sins. He said, *"As Moses lifted up the serpent in the wilderness, even so must the Son of Man be lifted up"* (John 3:14). Jesus paid a debt He didn't owe because we owed a debt we couldn't pay. His one sacrificial act changed the meaning of the word "Calvary" forever. The One who died there can change the meaning of your life.

"O the love that drew salvation's plan, oh the grace that brought it down to man; oh the mighty gulf that God did span at Calvary"

— Joseph Scriven

CAPERNAUM

Opportunities Lost; Misery Found

Lord Kenneth Clark, internationally known for his television series *Civilisation*, lived and died without faith in Jesus Christ. He admitted that he had been given many opportunities to believe; he rejected them all.

One of Jesus' parables teaches this obvious truth: if you have been given much, much will be required of

NAME: "Village of Nahum"
LOCATION: 85 miles N of Jerusalem, p.33
IDENTIFICATION: Jesus' headquarters for His Galilean ministry
STORY LINE: One of three cities cursed by Jesus for unbelief
READ IT IN THE BIBLE: Luke 10:1–20

you (Luke 12:48). Three Galilean villages knew this even better than Lord Clark.

Much of Jesus' ministry was centered on or around the Sea of Galilee. On the lake's northwest shore was Capernaum. The name means "village of Nahum," although it is impossible to know if the town's name specifically refers to Nahum the prophet. Capernaum was adopted by Jesus after His own city, Nazareth, rejected Him. He performed many miracles there including the healing of the centurion's servant (Matthew 8:5), the healing of Peter's mother–in–law (Mark 1:31), and the exorcism of an unclean spirit (Luke 4:33). But the city still largely rejected Jesus and His ministry.

This is where the principle of "much given, much required" applies. Jesus pronounced misery and despair on the people of three neighboring cities, Capernaum, Chorazin, and Bethsaida, because they had witnessed much of His ministry and yet chose not to believe.

Take some time today to pray for those who have heard the Gospel often, but still have rejected it. All without the Savior are lost, but some face greater punishment because they have had greater opportunity. They need our prayers most of all.

D' Arke des Verbonds

't Reuck Altaer

De Coningh Salomon

't Auteur des Brant-Offers

Verklaringe der
CYFER GETALEN

De Cypere Zee

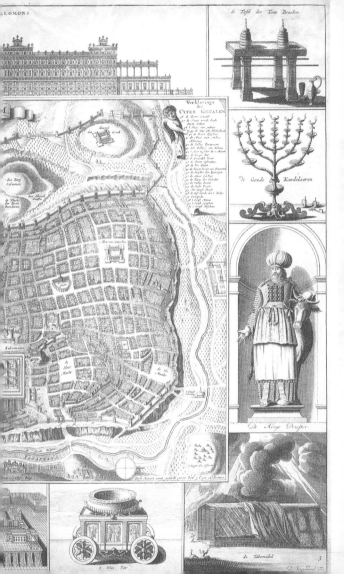

LOMONS.

de Tafel der Toon Brooden

Verklaringe der CYFER GETALEN

De Goude Kandelaeren

De Hooge Priester

de Tabernakel

3

MOUNT CARMEL

Let Your Faith Grow

In 1066 William, Duke of Normandy, faced formidable odds as he invaded England. But the Duke had one small advantage—a new invention called the stirrup. His soldiers could use the stirrup to fight from horseback, and that small tool aided the conquest of Britain.

NAME: "Garden" or "Orchard"
LOCATION: Near Israel's northern coast, p.33
IDENTIFICATION: 20–mile long range of mountains along Mediterranean Sea
STORY LINE: Faith begins with a cloud no larger than a man's hand
READ IT IN THE BIBLE: 1 Kings 18:1–46

The Bible compares faith to the tiniest of things, too. In the New Testament, Jesus likened faith to a grain of mustard seed, small in size but powerful in potential. In the Old Testament, faith was described like a tiny cloud.

The prophet Elijah beat the prophets of Baal on Carmel, a mountainous ridge that extends about twenty miles along the Mediterranean Sea. "Carmel" is a contraction of a Hebrew word meaning "vineyard" or "garden of God." Still heavily forested today, from Carmel's height of 1,742 feet you have an incredible view of the Jezreel Valley below.

After disposing of the pagan prophets, Elijah turned his attention to a crippling drought. It had been three years since the last rainfall, yet Elijah believed God's promise of rain on the way. The prophet sent his servant to the western edge of Carmel to see if any clouds were coming. None. Seven times the servant was sent back, and finally the man reported a cloud about the size of a man's hand. That was it. God came through. The small cloud soon grew and ruptured into a heavy downpour as God had promised.

Does your faith sometimes appear as just a small cloud? Remember that the promises of God are better than money in the bank. They always come true. So let your faith grow in proportion to His promises.

COLOSSE

Big People from Little Places

My father pastored a small church in Pennsylvania. When I was a teenager he challenged our church to send the whole youth group to a conference. The elders set rigorous standards that the two dozen of us in the youth group had to meet to have our way paid. But

NAME: "Garden" or "Orchard"
LOCATION: 110 miles E of Ephesus, p.12
IDENTIFICATION: Wool trading center at crossroads of Ephesus and the East
STORY LINE: Small church produced exceptional servants of the Lord
READ IT IN THE BIBLE: Colossians 4:1–18; Philemon 1–25

when it came time to pay up, the group had grown to sixty–six teens who qualified. It nearly bankrupted the church, but more than a third of those teens have spent a lifetime in ministry service to the Lord.

Sometimes God finds choice servants in out–of–the–way places. Amos was a sheepbreeder from Tekoa (Amos 1:1). William Carey, a cobbler from

Northampton, England, became "the father of modern missions."

Colosse was more than a hundred miles inland from the coastal city of Ephesus. Herodotus records that when the Persian king Xerxes came to Colosse, it was a city of great size. But by the time Paul wrote his epistle to the Colossians five hundred years later, the village was pretty much on the edge of nowhere.

Still Epaphras, who visited Paul in Rome and later was imprisoned with him (Philemon 1:23), was from Colosse. So were Philemon, Apphia, Archippus, and Onesimus, the slave who became a Christian (Philemon 16).

You might not be from New York City or L.A., but you can be used greatly of the Lord. The key to usability is to have clean hands and a pure heart (Psalm 24:3–4). If you take care of that, God will take care of using you.

CORINTH

Struggling Against Temptation

The Christians of Corinth were having trouble maturing in their faith. The apostle Paul preached at Corinth, planted a church there, and wrote at least two letters to these Christians. Still, the church of Corinth struggled.

NAME: "Ornament"
LOCATION: SW of Athens, p.12
IDENTIFICATION: Flourishing trade center at entrance to the Peloponnesus
STORY LINE: Paul planted a church here but struggled to mature it
READ IT IN THE BIBLE: 1 Corinthians 3:1–17

Two geographical features contributed to their spiritual battle, as these features drew many thousands of carnally minded visitors.

First, Corinth was near the isthmus that separates the Peloponnesian Peninsula from mainland Greece. Only four miles separate the Saronic Gulf on the Aegean Sea from the Corinthian Gulf on the Adriatic Sea. Because it was too dangerous to sail around the

Peloponnesus, as early as the sixth century B.C. ships would be lifted out of the water in one gulf, dragged overland on the Diolkos, a stone–paved roadway, and placed back in the water at the other gulf. During the Diolkos layover, rowdy sailors could hit town.

Corinth also was overshadowed by the 1,800–foot high outcrop of rock known as the Acrocorinth. On top of the Acrocorinth was the temple of Aphrodite. As many as a thousand temple prostitutes were reported to have been a part of the cult there. It was amazing how "religious" those sailors became while their ships were being dragged over the Diolkos. The sin on top of the Acrocorinth came oozing down into the city and into the church. Little wonder the Christians at Corinth struggled with carnality.

Sometimes you can't help being in places of temptation, but that doesn't mean you have to give in to it. Ask God to help you grow in grace and the knowledge of the Lord so you are prepared to win your spiritual struggles.

CYRENE

When God Puts the Pieces Together

I never cease to be amazed at how God brings people from all over the world together, at the right time and in the right place, to accomplish His will. Consider this . . .

Cyrene was a city on the coast of North Africa, just north of modern Benghazi, Libya. It was founded in

NAME: "Ornament"
LOCATION: N coast of Africa, p.12
IDENTIFICATION: Libyan city that was capital of Cyrenaica in North Africa
STORY LINE: From here came Simon who carried Jesus' cross to Calvary
READ IT IN THE BIBLE: Matthew 27:15–37

630 B.C. by a Dorian colony from Thera, Greece, and named after the spring Kyre. The chief city between Egypt and Carthage in Tunisia, Cyrene was conquered by Alexander the Great in 331 B.C., and it became a Roman colony in 74 B.C. The people of Cyrene were dark–skinned but lighter than sub–Saharan Africans.

A hundred thousand Jews from Palestine had been

settled in Cyrene by Ptolemy Soter (B.C. 323–285), and by New Testament times the Jewish community there was even larger. One member of that community was named Simon. Simon of Cyrene was visiting Jerusalem during the Passover feast when suddenly there was a commotion in the streets. He watched as the crowd swelled and Roman soldiers escorted a man along the Via Dolorosa to Golgotha, the place of crucifixion. Suddenly and unexpectedly, the soldiers compelled Simon to carry Jesus' cross for Him.

When Simon left his home to come to Jerusalem, he couldn't have dreamed what God had in store for him. Neither can you. God may have something special in mind for you, but only if, like Simon, you are pliable in His hand, faithful in His vineyard, and active in pursuing a life of worshiping Him. Don't just sit back and wait for God to move in your life. Start moving for God and watch what He will do.

DAMASCUS

Welcoming the Enemy

Imagine these scenarios. Little Red Riding Hood is told that the Big Bad Wolf has had a change of heart and wants to be her best friend. Or what about this? Adolf Hitler has realized his hatred for the Jews was wrong and wants to join B'nai B'rith.

NAME: "Silent is the Sackcloth Weaver"
LOCATION: 160 miles NE of Israel, pp.13 & 33
IDENTIFICATION: Capital city of Syria situated on major trade routes
STORY LINE: Here Saul presented himself as a new convert to Christ
READ IT IN THE BIBLE: Acts 9:1–25

If you're at all skeptical about these scenarios, you understand how Ananias, a Christian in Damascus, felt when he was told to receive Saul of Tarsus as a brother in Christ.

The capital of Syria, Damascus is protected on three sides by mountains. It's in a particularly fertile area, watered by two rivers, the Nahr Barada (biblical Abana) and the Nahr el–A waj (biblical Pharpar). Together the two rivers irrigate four hundred square miles of land around Damascus.

About A.D. 35, Saul was traveling to this fertile area in his zealous persecution of Christians. But on the road to Damascus, a heavenly light blinded him, and Saul met the Lord in the miracle of salvation. By the time he arrived in the city, a Christian named Ananias had already received instructions from the Lord to seek out Saul and assist him in regaining his sight. Naturally, at first Ananias was reticent. But Saul's life had been radically changed by God's grace, so Ananias called him "Brother Saul" (Acts 9:17).

When people who are different from you come to church, do you have difficulty welcoming them? What about those whose lifestyles were especially ungodly before they came to Christ? Whatever they were is not what they are. If their hearts have changed toward God, ask Him to change your heart toward them.

CITY OF DAVID

Small Beginnings

In 1948 Dick McDonald started a restaurant in California. Ray Kroc started the first franchise for the fast–food restaurant in 1955, kept the original name, and you know the rest of the story.

NAME: "City of David"

LOCATION: South side of Jerusalem, p.53

IDENTIFICATION: The old Jebusite stronghold captured by David and his men

STORY LINE: David made Jerusalem his political, religious, and economic capital

READ IT IN THE BIBLE: 2 Samuel 5:1–12

"*Who has despised the day of small things?*" (Zechariah 4:10). Small things should never be taken lightly, because big things grow from small things. Nobody knew that better than David.

The story of how David's men took a Jebusite stronghold by climbing up through a water shaft is fascinating. What they captured from the Jebusites, however, was not the city of Jerusalem but a narrow strip of land on the steep eastern slope of Mount Zion. The east side has a steep slope of about 60 degrees. Excavations from 1978 to 1985 by the late Professor Yigal Shiloh confirmed a group of stone walls filled in with earth and stones forming the terraces upon which the houses of David's fortress–city were built.

Often in the Old Testament the "City of David" refers to Jerusalem in general. In the New Testament it frequently means Bethlehem, the city of David's birth. But when the "City of David" was first mentioned in the Bible, it referred to nothing but a small hillside now engulfed by the larger city of Jerusalem.

If you feel like your contribution to the cause of Christ is small like the original city of David, don't despise the day of small things. It's from the solid foundation of small service that God builds much larger service. Take heart. The city David knew was not the large and glorious Jerusalem of today. Still, it was a place to begin.

DEAD SEA

A Modern Ecological Disaster

The Dead Sea is a modern day ecological disaster. This large saltwater lake, frequently called the "Salt Sea" or "Sea of Arabah" in the Bible, is rapidly disappearing. Irrigation both in Jordan and Israel have produced over–extraction of water from the Jordan River, the

NAME: "Dead Sea"
LOCATION: 12 miles SE of Jerusalem, p.33
IDENTIFICATION: Known as "The Salt Sea" in the Bible, the lowest spot on the earth's surface
STORY LINE: Abundant minerals made the Dead Sea a historic treasure
READ IT IN THE BIBLE: Ezekiel 47:1–12; Joshua 3:1–17

main water source for the Dead Sea. The sea lies in the Jordan Valley and is the lowest spot on earth, more than 1,300 feet below sea level and getting lower every year.

The water of the Dead Sea is 27 percent minerals at the southern end. Down to about 130 feet, the sea water comprises about 300 grams of salt per kilogram of seawater. That's ten times saltier than the oceans.

Below 300 feet the Dead Sea is literally so saturated with salt that it piles up on the sea bottom. Nothing grows in the sea. The water is deadly to almost all living things. Fish accidentally swimming into the Dead Sea waters are killed instantly.

Still, at En Gedi, on the sea's western shore, the prophet Ezekiel foresaw a time when even the salty waters of the Dead Sea would be re–created and the deadly sea would teem with fish (Ezekiel 47:1–12; compare Zechariah 14:8).

Such is the regenerating power of God. If God can take the harshest place on the planet, heal its waters, and restore it to one of the greatest fishing holes in the world, imagine what He can do with you. No life is so depleted of meaning that God cannot make it worthwhile. What He will do with the Dead Sea, He can do with you. God makes all things beautiful in their time (Ecclesiastes 3:11).

EASTERN GATE

Just Inside the Eastern Gate

There's an old hymn of comfort that promises, "I will meet you in the morning / Just inside the Eastern Gate / Then be ready, faithful pilgrim / Lest with you it be too late."

NAME: "Eastern Gate"
LOCATION: At Jerusalem's eastern wall, p.53
IDENTIFICATION: One of the nine gates into the "Old City" of Jerusalem
STORY LINE: Through this gate one day will come the Prince and Messiah
READ IT IN THE BIBLE: Ezekiel 43:1–44:3

"Just inside the Eastern Gate" is a spiritual reference to heaven, but the real Eastern Gate is the most important and impressive gate in Jerusalem. Also known as the Beautiful Gate, it is located near the middle of the city's eastern wall. Built just north of the altar in Solomon's temple, it was the main entrance to the temple that Jesus often used.

In A.D. 810 the Arabs walled up the Eastern Gate

and it has remained closed ever since. Because Jewish people believe the Prince or Messiah will enter Jerusalem through this gate (Ezekiel 43:1–44:3), when Suleiman the Magnificent rebuilt the gates in A.D. 1539–42 he placed a Moslem graveyard in front of it. Suleiman knew the Messiah was a Nazarite who could not have contact with the dead and so would not pass through the cemetery. But Suleiman was too late. The Messiah had already gone through the gate, riding on a donkey, with the people of Jerusalem shouting, *"'Hosanna! Blessed is He who comes in the name of the Lord'"* (Mark 11:1–11).

Entering the Eastern Gate has become symbolic of entering into the heaven that Jesus is preparing for those who love Him. If you have friends or family who are now with the Lord, may the final stanza of Isaiah Martin's hymn "The Eastern Gate" bring you comfort today. "If you hasten off to Glory / Linger near the Eastern Gate; For I'm coming in the morning / So you'll not have long to wait."

EDEN

Where It All Began

What do Kitty Hawk, Bologna, and Eden have in common? They were places of great beginnings. Kitty Hawk, North Carolina, was where the Wright brothers flew their first airplane in 1903 and gave us crowded airports, flight delays, and space travel. In 1895, at his

NAME: "Delight"
LOCATION: Likely in modern Iraq, p.13
IDENTIFICATION: The primal site where where God placed Adam and Eve
STORY LINE: In the most idyllic setting, man disobeyed God
READ IT IN THE BIBLE: Genesis 2:1–25

father's country estate near Bologna, Italy, Guglielmo Marconi succeeded in sending wireless signals over a distance of one and a half miles; the result was top 40 countdowns, talk radio, and Bible teaching that has changed the world. And Eden is where everything began.

Genesis 2:8 says *"The LORD God planted a garden eastward in Eden, and there He put the man whom He had formed.*" Eden was a lovely garden where flora and fauna of every kind abounded. The tree of life was there, as was the tree of the knowledge of good and evil. A river flowed through Eden, and the ground was rich in precious minerals. Eden was paradise, a place of peace and tranquility, until Satan and sin entered it.

Eden is where it all began, and where it was all lost. Paradise lost. What the first Adam lost through disobedience, Jesus, the Last Adam, regained through obedience. Adam brought the curse of sin to all who are born from him, but Jesus brought the blessing of salvation to all who are born again in Him (Romans 5:12–21). Eden was the place it all began; Calvary was the place it all began again. We don't need to return to Eden, but we do all need to come to the foot of the cross. That's where we get our one and only chance to begin again.

Then the LORD said to him, "Take your sandals off your feet, for the place where you stand is holy ground."

ACTS 7:33

EDOM

Stubborn Resistance

Edom will forever be remembered as the nation that stubbornly resisted God. Unfortunately, some people will be remembered for the same thing.

Edom is the high plateau to the southeast of the Dead Sea. The name is not mentioned in the genealogy

NAME: "Red"
LOCATION: SE of Israel, pp.13 &33
IDENTIFICATION: High plateau SE of the Dead Sea, home of Esau's descendants
STORY LINE: Edom refused Israel passage on their way to Canaan
READ IT IN THE BIBLE: Numbers 20:14–21

in Genesis 10, but it first appears in the story of Esau in Genesis 25:30. Esau was called Edom from the red color of the stew for which he sold his birthright to Jacob. The Edom plateau rises to over five thousand feet. Dark red sandstone cliffs form its western flank. From there the land falls sharply into the Arabah, the deep depression in which the Dead Sea lies.

Although the land of Edom was generally inhospitable, its wealth came largely from the caravan trade that brought goods from India and South Arabia to the Mediterranean coast and Egypt. The important King's Highway (Numbers 21:22) passed through Edom. The Israelites had been using the King's Highway as they approached the Promised Land from the south and east, but the king of Edom refused to allow them passage. That resulted in the long history of enmity between Judah and Edom. Many prophets spoke against Edom, including Isaiah (Isaiah 11:14), Ezekiel (Ezekiel 32:29), Joel (Joel 3:19), Amos (Amos 1:11–12), and Malachi (Malachi 1:2–4).

Edom's relationship with God was soured through foolish obstinacy. Often that's true of people as well. The best way to win God's favor is to get to know Him (Jeremiah 9:23–24) and to let Him shape your life as a potter gently shapes the clay. True happiness is found in fellowship with God, not in stubborn resistance toward Him.

EGYPT

Sleeping With An Elephant

My friends from Canada refer to their relationship with the United States as "sleeping with an elephant." The prominence of the United States clearly makes being a Canadian a challenge.

NAME: "Land of the Copts"
LOCATION: SW of Israel, p.13
IDENTIFICATION: The major foreign power interacting with Israel
STORY LINE: For 430 years, Egypt was the Hebrews' involuntary home
READ IT IN THE BIBLE: Exodus 12:1–42

Israel felt the same way about Egypt. Until the Six–Day War in 1967, Israel almost continuously lived in the shadow of Egypt. With a long and rich history dating back millennia before Christ, many biblical events took place in Egypt. Abraham lived there during a famine (Genesis 12:10). Joseph was sold to Egyptians, and his whole family joined him there after he became an Egyptian leader (Genesis 37–50). The Hebrews were enslaved there after Joseph died (Exodus 1:6–11). Moses was born and raised there (Exodus 2:1–10). God led the Hebrews out of Egypt to the Promised Land (Exodus 12:31–42).

Egypt grew up around the Nile River. The ancient historian Herodotus called Egypt "the gift of the Nile." The Nile provides Egypt, which is primarily desert, with its only source of fresh water for crop irrigation. Little wonder Egyptians worshipped the Nile and why, when the God of Israel needed to convince the powerful Pharaoh to release His people, the Nile became a primary target for a display of divine power.

In the Bible, Egypt is often a symbol for sin from which deliverance is found only in the power of God. If you are facing your own "Egypt" today and are having trouble breaking free from the power of some elephant–sized sin, ask God to deliver you the way He did the ancient Israelites. The power of Egypt is no match for the power of God.

ELAH

Fighting the Giants in Your Life

In 1314, a small army led by Robert the Bruce fought against the mighty forces of King Edward II at Bannockburn. In 490 B.C., Persian King Darius lost against a handful of Greek soldiers at the Battle of Marathon. But the most unequal of all land battles took place in the Valley of Elah.

NAME: "Oak"
LOCATION: 25 miles SW of Jerusalem, p.33
IDENTIFICATION: The southernmost valley of the Shephelah, one–half mile wide
STORY LINE: David defeated the Philistine giant Goliath here
READ IT IN THE BIBLE: 1 Samuel 17:1–51

Elah was the southernmost valley in the Shephelah, the sloping lowlands that began at Hebron and descended in a northerly then westerly direction toward the Mediterranean Sea. At the Wadi al–Sant, Elah forms a level valley about a half mile wide. Here Israel's armies camped on the northern hills, the Philistines were on the southern hills, and Israel was paralyzed with fear because the Philistine warrior Goliath stood nine-and-a-half feet tall.

When young David visited three of his older brothers in Saul's army and heard Goliath's threats, he was incensed, not paralyzed. He responded in faith, not in fear. *"Who is this uncircumcised Philistine, that he should defy the armies of the living God?"* (1 Samuel 17:26). David was outmatched in size, armor, and experience, but not in heart. It was not conventional armor that steeled his resolve but genuine faith in the power of God. He felled the giant with just a sling and a tiny stone.

The giants in our lives are no larger than the one in David's, but often we try to kill them with conventional wisdom or popular advice. That won't work. It's faith in God's power that defeats our giants. Ask Him to give you that faith today.

ELIM

Relying on God Isn't Always Easy

For the Jews, Egypt meant a life of slavery and ill–treatment. But when God delivered His people from Egyptian bondage, their song of praise quickly turned to a dirge of complaint. At Marah they found nothing but bitter water. The Lord showed Moses how to make

NAME: "Oaks"
LOCATION: The Arabian Desert, p.13
IDENTIFICATION: Desert oasis between Marah and the Desert of Sin
STORY LINE: Israel complained and God graciously provided
  READ IT IN THE BIBLE: Exodus 15:22–16:21

it drinkable. Then it was on to Elim where they found twelve wells of water and seventy palm trees. That was more like it.

But the Israelites missed the delicious meat and fresh–baked bread of Egypt, and their ungrateful hearts spewed out complaints to God. Israel's complaining only brought God's mercy. First, He rained down tiny drops of heavenly bread every morning except the Sabbath. Then He brought flocks of quail each evening so the people would have the meat and bread they craved. But God's mercy didn't mean a life of ease for Israel.

The manna was small, round, and about the size of a coriander seed, and it wasn't delivered in plastic bags. When manna fell to the earth, the Jews had to gather it up. Imagine gathering something as small as the head of a pin. What's worse, the manna was white, and it settled on the white sands of the desert. Sifting it from the sand would not be an easy task, but it was all they had.

Often it isn't easy to rely on God, but when God is all you have, the challenge of playing by His rules beats starving in the wilderness of sin. Think about it. Even if you must work hard at following God, it's still the sure path to blessing.

EMMAUS

Jesus Is Alive

I have visited the Holy Land each year since 1964, and one of my favorite sites is Emmaus. There's just something about Emmaus that quickens the heart of a Christian.

NAME: "Warm Wells"
LOCATION: 7 miles NW of Jerusalem, p.33
IDENTIFICATION: Likely El–Qubeibeh on the Roman Road passing Nebi Samwil
STORY LINE: Jesus encountered two disciples after His resurrection
READ IT IN THE BIBLE: Luke 24:1–27

On Resurrection Sunday, two of Jesus' disciples were returning to Emmaus after that tragic Passover weekend. One was Cleopas and the other person is unnamed. A stranger caught up with them along the way. Cleopas related all about the Crucifixion, the empty tomb, and how the disciples' hopes were now dashed. Jesus, their unrecognized companion, rebuked them and *"beginning at Moses and all the Prophets, He expounded to them in all the Scriptures the things concerning Himself"* (Luke 24:27). As they ate the evening meal together in Emmaus, the disciples finally recognized Jesus, and He vanished from their sight.

At least four sites have claimed to be biblical Emmaus. Colonia, about four miles west of Jerusalem, is on the main road to Joppa. Abu Ghosh is about nine miles west of Jerusalem and is identified with Old Testament Kiriath–jearim. Amwas is about twenty miles west of Jerusalem on the Jaffa road. The most likely site is El–Qubeibeh, about seven miles northwest of Jerusalem on a Roman road.

When Cleopas and his friend knew they had encountered Jesus, they immediately retraced their steps to Jerusalem to tell the others that Jesus was alive. The resurrection is the best news possible, and it still gives hope to the hopeless. Christians do not worship a dead Savior; we worship a living Lord. Jesus is alive.

EN GEDI

Honor the King

Have you noticed how nasty political campaigns have become? In the 2004 presidential election, the candidates stood just feet apart at the debates while they maligned the character and policies of the other.

SMALL CAPS Name: "Spring of the Goat"
Location: 35 miles SE of Jerusalem, p.33
Identification: A vital oasis on the west side of the Dead Sea
Story Line: David spares Saul's life out of deference to Saul's position
Read it in the Bible: 1 Samuel 24:1–22

When King Saul lost his grip on leadership because of disobedience to God, he often tried to kill David. But David would not retaliate. Was he just a weak political figure or was it something else?

Once David sought refuge from Saul at En Gedi, a green oasis on the west side of the Dead Sea. At En Gedi a hot water spring gushes from the limestone cliff. The oasis was famous for its palms, vineyards, and balsam (Song of Songs 1:14; Josephus *Antiquities* 20.1.2). While David was hiding in its recesses, the king entered the cave to answer the call of nature. David's men urged him to kill Saul, but instead he crept close to the king and cut off a corner of his robe. When Saul left, David called to the king, bowed to the ground, and pointed out that he spared Saul because, *"I will not stretch out my hand against my lord, for he is the LORD's anointed"* (1 Samuel 24:10). His respect for Saul's position as the God–appointed king would not permit David to malign Saul's character or take his life.

If we had a Romans 13:1 view of the God–ordained people in our government, whether good or bad, we'd have a very different tone in our political campaigns. Today, instead of complaining about your appointed leaders, pray for them and heed Peter's advice: *"Honor all people. Love the brotherhood. Fear God. Honor the king"* (1 Peter 2:17).

EPHESUS

Repent & Return

Repentance is the stepchild of the 21st century church. It's the missing ingredient in the quick and easy conversions seen today. The New Testament word for repentance means to change your mind so that your views, your values, and your lifestyle are completely

NAME: "Desirable"
LOCATION: Western shore of Turkey, p.12
IDENTIFICATION: Major city of Asia Minor during the New Testament years
STORY LINE: Paul creates an uproar when idol makers lose business
READ IT IN THE BIBLE: Acts 19:21–41; Revelation 2:1–7

different. Such drastic change is little expected and often missing from some current models of church growth.

Ephesus was a church in need of repentance. The major city of the Roman province of Asia Minor, Ephesus was built on a natural harbor whose waves, according to Pliny the Elder, "used to wash up to the temple of Diana." This temple, one of the seven wonders of the ancient world, was an impressive building supported on one hundred large columns. Paul's life was severely threatened when the city's Diana idol makers realized his preaching of repentance and salvation was a threat to their livelihood (Acts 19:24, 30–31). According to Bishop Irenaeus of the second century, the apostle John lived in Ephesus both before and after his exile on the island of Patmos (Revelation 1:9).

In John's message to the seven churches of Revelation, the apostle commended the Christians of Ephesus but called on them to repent and return to their first works if they wanted the continued blessing of God. Repent and return—it might sound difficult, but it's the only way to come back once you've lost your way. If you've gotten off track in your walk with the Lord, don't see repentance as an inconvenience; see it as a lifesaver. A change of mind and behavior is the way back to the heart of God and to His blessing. Make it your way today.

EUPHRATES

The One to Watch

Of all the great rivers of the world—the Nile, the
Mississippi, the Yangtze, the Tiber, the Amazon—
perhaps none has as much relevance to history past,
present, or future as the Euphrates.

NAME: "Break Forth"
LOCATION: Turkey, Syria, Iraq, p.13
IDENTIFICATION: A major river that flowed out of the Garden of Eden
STORY LINE: River will dry up allowing kings of the East to
    march on Israel
READ IT IN THE BIBLE: Revelation 16:1–21

The Euphrates is the largest river in western Asia,
flowing some 1,800 miles in a southeasterly direction
from Armenia to the Persian Gulf. At Korna, about
100 miles from the gulf, it joins with the Tigris River.
The Euphrates was one of four rivers branching from
the Garden of Eden (Genesis 2:14). In antiquity, it was
called *"the river"* (Deuteronomy 11:24) or *"the great
river"* (Joshua 1:4).

Today the Euphrates is front page news again. Although Baghdad is built on the Tigris, the recent Iraq War often focused our attention on the Euphrates, only thirty miles to the west and the site of insurgent trouble spots like Najaf, Ramadi, and Nasiriya.

History future will return the Euphrates to center stage again. In the Book of Revelation, when the sixth vial of God's judgment is poured out on the river, the water will be dried up to prepare for an invasion of Israel by the armies of the East, perhaps a reference to China, Japan, or even India. This initiates the final world conflict known as the battle of Armageddon.

The Euphrates River is a constant reminder that we know how the story ends. Be encouraged. The long war against God is futile and will end when *the kingdoms of this world have become the kingdoms of our Lord and of His Christ, and He shall reign forever and ever!"* (Revelation 11:15).

EZION GEBER

When Things Get Out of Control

I grew up in western Pennsylvania in the glory days of U.S. Steel. In my hometown, if you didn't work in a steel mill, you didn't work. My father–in–law was a crane man over the open hearth that melted large vats

NAME: "Backbone of a Man"
LOCATION: 160 miles S of Jerusalem, pp.13 & 33
IDENTIFICATION: An industrial port at the head of the Gulf of Aqaba
STORY LINE: Solomon carried on a profitable commerce from here
READ IT IN THE BIBLE: 1 Kings 9:1–28

of steel. I can appreciate why archaeologist Nelson Glueck called Ezion Geber "the Pittsburgh of Palestine."

Ezion Geber was Solomon's vital seaport at the head of the Gulf of Aqaba, which extended north from the Red Sea. From here, Solomon and Hiram, king of Tyre, carried on profitable commercial ventures. Solomon mined copper just fifteen miles to the north at Timna and brilliantly positioned huge smelting factories at

Ezion Geber to catch the prevailing winds to fire his blast furnaces. The merchant ships of Tarshish made a round trip every three years from Ezion Geber to ports along the coasts of Africa, Arabia, and the East bringing gold from Ophir, silver, ivory, apes, and monkeys (1 Kings 10:22).

Today Ezion Geber is gone. The copper smelters have been replaced by wind surfers and scuba divers. Ezion Geber is now Eliat, the southern water playground of Israel. Ezion Geber is a reminder of what the human spirit can achieve, but also of how fleeting our accomplishments can be. Just as big steel has all but vanished from Pittsburgh, the once mighty Ezion Geber has vanished from Israel. Little wonder Jesus said, *"Do not lay up for yourselves treasures on earth, where moth and rust destroy and where thieves break in and steal . . . For where your treasure is, there your heart will be also"* (Matthew 6:19–21). That's good advice for us today.

FAIR HAVENS

Be Careful When Things Are Going Well

Author Judith Viorst wrote a humorous book for children called *Alexander and the Terrible, Horrible, No Good, Very Bad Day*. The apostle Paul had a string of such bad days, and they weren't funny at all.

NAME: "Suitable Port"
LOCATION: S coast of Crete, p.12
IDENTIFICATION: A small harbor near Lasea on the Island of Crete
STORY LINE: Paul's ship sought shelter from the Mediterranean winds here
READ IT IN THE BIBLE: Acts 27:1–44

After two years in jail at Caesarea, Paul exercised his right as a Roman citizen to demand a trial before Caesar. So, King Agrippa shipped him off to Italy. The first day they covered a distance of seventy miles to Sidon. But the second day northwesterly winds meant slow going. They put in at Myra on the southern coast of modern Turkey. It then took them several days to sail the 130 miles to Cnidus. Finally they made for the open sea and the harbor of Fair Havens, a small seaport on Crete's south coast.

It was October. Navigation across the open seas was already unsafe. Should they spend the winter in Fair Havens or sail another forty miles to the better harbor at Phoenix? Paul admonished them to stay, but *"when the south wind blew softly"* (Acts 27:13) they took a chance. How wrong they were. They were fooled by the gentle, warm winds from the south. Soon the wind shifted and they faced a Euroclydon, a "northeaster" of gale force. Their decision to sail led to a disastrous shipwreck.

It's like that in life too. When the winds blow softly, we must be the most alert to the attacks of Satan. We become less vigilant when things are going our way. That makes us vulnerable. If you're running on a spiritual high today, be alert. Don't take anything for granted. Ask God to help you navigate the troubled waters ahead.

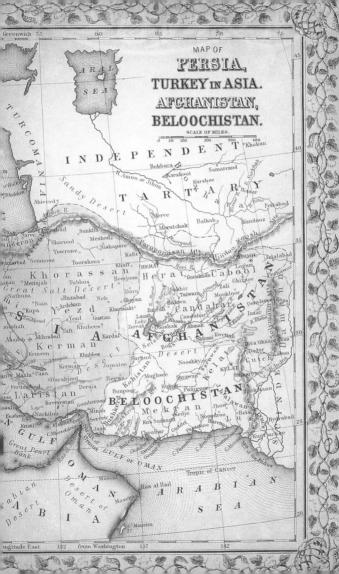

MAP OF
PERSIA,
TURKEY IN ASIA.
AFGHANISTAN,
BELOOCHISTAN.

SCALE OF MILES.

0   50   100   200   300   400

ARAL SEA

TURCOMANIA

INDEPENDENT TARTARY

Sandy Desert

Bokhara
Karakool
Kurshee
Samarcand
Hissar
Feizabad
Kundooz
Balkah
Merutchak
Merve

Hindoo-Koosh Mts
Paropomisan Mts

Khorassan
Great Salt Desert
Merinjab
Mahtunz
Nain
Ardekan
Yezd
Neh
Ghayan
Khurmaki
Gustan
Tubbus
Dara
HERAT
Herat
Heri Rood

Caboul
Gurakhan
Zali
Ghizne
Mookloor
Peshawur
Dera Ismael Khan
Jelalabad

CABOOL

AFGHANISTAN

Kerman
Khubbes
Desert
Sexved
Lake Zurrah
Khash
Dhoshak
Ahmad
Candahar
Shiram
Kwettah

Larristan
Ferizabad
Deraia
Regan
Pumgoor
Nooshky
Sarawan
Kelat Ghuzee
Dadur
KELAT
Shikarpoor
Cutch

BELOOCHISTAN

Mekran
Kedjie
Jhow
Jhalawan
Bela
Hyderabad

PERSIAN GULF

Great Pearl Bank

OMAN

GULF OF OMAN

Muscat
Ras al Had
Masera

Tropic of Cancer

Desert of Omana

ARABIA

ARABIAN SEA

C. Murcira

Longitude East 132   from Washington 137   142

FULLER'S FIELD

The Immanuel Sign

The story of King Ahaz of Judah is so important that it was recorded in three Old Testament books. To get some insight into Ahaz, read 2 Chronicles 28:1–6, 16–25 and 2 Kings 16:1–9 before you read Isaiah 7:1–14.

NAME: "Trample"
LOCATION: South side of Jerusalem
IDENTIFICATION: A field near Jerusalem where launderers cleaned clothes
STORY LINE: Isaiah met King Ahaz here to announce the virgin birth
READ IT IN THE BIBLE: Isaiah 7:1–14

When King Ahaz was being attacked by a coalition of forces from Israel and Syria, he foolishly made an alliance with Assyria, his sworn enemy, rather than seek the Lord's help. The prophet Isaiah arranged to meet the king near the Fuller's Field just outside Jerusalem's southern walls, probably because he knew no one would be hanging out there. Fullers were launderers; they cleaned clothes, removing stains by stomping the garments with their feet in a pool of water containing an alkaline substance. The whole process was pretty smelly, so fullers were obliged to work outside the gates. The field was probably close to En–rogel ("Spring of the Fuller").

Isaiah encouraged Ahaz to ask a sign from Jehovah to prove He would keep His promises and would deliver His people. Ahaz refused. So Isaiah informed him that God would give His own sign, a once–for–all sign that He is the God who saves. This was the remarkable sign: *"Behold, the virgin shall conceive and bear a Son, and you shall call His name Immanuel"* (Isaiah 7:14).

What does Christmas mean to you? Does it mean more than presents? Does it mean that you trust God to keep His promises? It should. The promise of a virgin giving birth to a Son is the sign that you can trust your uncertain future to a certain God. He is the great Promise Keeper.

GABBATHA

Facing Decisions with Courage

After the terrorist attacks of September 11, 2001, Pat Tillman left his lucrative career with the NFL's Arizona Cardinals to enlist in the U.S. Army. This brave soldier was killed by friendly fire in Afghanistan.

NAME: "Height"
LOCATION: NE Jerusalem, p.53
IDENTIFICATION: Area in Pilate's palace where he pronounced judgments
STORY LINE: Pilate presided over Jesus' trial from the Gabbatha
READ IT IN THE BIBLE: John 18:28–19:16

Contrast the Pat Tillman story with Pilate's story. Pontius Pilate was the governor of Judea from A.D. 26–36. He presided over the trial of Jesus.

When the Sanhedrin brought Jesus to the Praetorium, Pilate didn't want to get involved (John 18:31). But he questioned Jesus and announced, *"I find no fault in Him at all"* (John 18:38). After scourging Him, Pilate presented God's sinless Son to the mob who demanded,

"Crucify Him." The governor said, *"Why, what evil has He done?"* (Matthew 27:23). But the crowd prevailed. Surrendering to the mob, Pilate washed his hands and said, *"I am innocent of the blood of this just Person"* (Matthew 27:24).

Finally, Pilate brought Jesus out to the judgment seat, a place called The Pavement, or in Hebrew, "Gabbatha" (John 19:13). In Greek the word means "paved with stones." It was the raised platform before the palace in Jerusalem where formal sentencing by the governor took place. Here, the gutless Pilate handed over the innocent Jesus to be crucified.

Pilate will forever be remembered as a coward. Eusebius reports that he ultimately committed suicide during the reign of the emperor Caligula (*History 2.7*).

When faced with a decision that takes uncommon courage, we all have two choices. We can be like Pat or we can be like Pilate. Claim this promise: *"Wait on the LORD; be of good courage, and He shall strengthen your heart"* (Psalm 27:14).

GADARA

Deviled Ham

In the movie *Nate and Hayes,* pirates of the South Pacific found haven in a strange place called Panape. It was unusually cold there, a place where good people never went. Gadara was like that.

NAME: "Walls"

LOCATION: 6 miles SE of Sea of Galilee, p.33

IDENTIFICATION: A chief city of the Decapolis, north of the Yarmuk River

STORY LINE: Jesus cast demons from a hapless man into a herd of swine

READ IT IN THE BIBLE: Mark 5:1–20

Located five miles southeast of the Sea of Galilee, Gadara was on "the other side," the side of the sea that was wild and untamed, riddled with caves that were filled with demon–possessed people.

One day Jesus and His disciples sailed *"to the other side of the sea, to the country of the Gadarenes"* (Mark 5:1). A demonic man stormed down the hillside, probably intending to scare the living daylights out of those in the boat. The man was pathetic. Demons so controlled him that he cut himself with stones and cried out day and night. He had often broken the chains that were meant to bind him. No one could tame him. But Jesus changed all that. The Savior calmly cast multiple demons out of the man and, at their request, into a herd of swine. Two thousand crazed pigs ran into the sea and drowned.

When the townspeople came out to see what was happening, they found the pathetic man sitting at the feet of Jesus, fully clothed and in his right mind (Mark 5:15). That's always the way it is when we meet Jesus in a meaningful way. We are completely changed. We are clothed with His righteousness. And for the first time in our lives, we are in our right minds.

Don't be afraid to encounter Jesus today. Jesus will change your life for the better, like He did for the man living "on the other side."

GALATIA

When You Lose the Joy of Your Salvation

Do you remember the day you were saved? How exciting that day was. No longer did you feel guilty for disobeying God's law. For the first time you knew you would go to heaven when you die. There was nothing to compare to it. But what about now? Have you lost your joy?

NAME: "Land of the Gauls"
LOCATION: Central Turkey, p.13
IDENTIFICATION: Roman province in Asia Minor inhabited by invading Gauls
STORY LINE: The Galatian churches reverted from grace to the Law
READ IT IN THE BIBLE: Galatians 1:1–24

Paul sensed the Galatians had lost the joy of their salvation because of legalism. The Galatians had always been invaders. Perhaps you know them as the Gauls or Celts. They sacked Rome in 390 B.C., but when they attempted to conquer Greece, they were repelled. So they turned to Asia Minor and settled in what today is Turkey. In 25 B.C. Galatia became a Roman province. Paul passed through there on all three of his missionary journeys. But despite Paul's repeated presence, from his letter to the Galatians it evident that the believers there were losing their joy to the pressures of legalism.

Legalism is when Christians revert to keeping the Law rather than living by grace. A group of Jewish teachers had passed through Galatia insisting that non–Jewish believers must obey Jewish law and keep the traditional rules. But we cannot be saved by keeping the law. We are saved by God's grace and must live by His grace (Ephesians 2:8–10). Legalism stresses performance over our relationship with God through Christ Jesus. It causes us to feel guilty because we fall short of others' expectations.

If you are feeling guilty and inadequate today, check your focus. Are you living by faith in Christ or by trying to live up to the demands of others? Don't let legalism rob you of your joy.

GALILEE

Your Speech Betrays You

I was born and raised just north of Pittsburgh, Pennsylvania. While growing up I learned to speak "Pittsburghese" and would say things like, "You'ns better read up the room before you watch the Stillers game." (You'd better clean the room before you watch

> NAME: "Circle" or "District"
> LOCATION: Northern Israel, p.33
> IDENTIFICATION: Boyhood home of Jesus and the site of most of His ministry
> STORY LINE: Peter's Galilean accent exposed his association with Jesus
> READ IT IN THE BIBLE: Mark 14:53–72

the Steelers game.) Alas, having been away from western Pennsylvania since high school, I've lost most of that delightful accent.

It's odd how much an accent identifies a person. Nobody knew that better than Peter. He was born in Galilee, the land bordered on the east by the upper Jordan River and the Sea of Galilee. To the south was the plain of Esdraelon. The western boundary followed the Mediterranean Sea to Mount Carmel. Although the people of Galilee were mostly Jewish by faith, they came from various ethnic backgrounds. The influence of this racial diversity caused the speech of the Galileans to be different from those in southern Palestine.

On the night that Jesus was betrayed, Peter followed Him at a distance. One of the servant girls at Caiaphas' house saw Peter warming himself by the fire and identified him as a follower of Jesus. He denied it. A second time she identified Peter and again he denied it. Finally someone from the crowd shouted, *"Surely you are one of them; for you are a Galilean, and your speech shows it"* (Mark 14:70).

How about your speech? Does it show that you are a follower of Jesus? Not your accent, but the way you speak, the things you say, and the way you say them. Let your speech be a verbal magnet to draw your friends to the Savior.

GATH

When Things Get Out of Control

Harriet Beecher Stowe (1811–1896) grew up in a godly home. Both her father and brother were pastors. While living in Cincinnati, Ohio, she saw firsthand the cruelties of slavery. In 1851 she wrote *Uncle Tom's Cabin,* the novel that became the rallying point for the anti–slavery movement.

NAME: "Winepress"
LOCATION: 42 miles SW of Jerusalem, p.33
IDENTIFICATION: One of five chief cities of the Philistines, home of Goliath
STORY LINE: The residents of Gath will laugh when Israel is punished
READ IT IN THE BIBLE: Micah 1:1–16

Social concern for the oppressed has a long history. Micah prophesied both to Israel and Judah and predicted ruin for all nations and leaders who oppressed others. In his day, the upper classes exploited the poor, but no one was speaking out or doing anything to stop it.

Although Micah predicted the destruction of

Samaria and Jerusalem, he cautioned the people not to speak publicly about this impending judgment because their enemies would rub it in. *"Tell it not in Gath. Weep not at all,"* Micah counsels, *"Roll yourself in the dust"* (Micah 1:10). Gath was one of the five chief cities of the Philistines in the Shephelah, the lower foothills of Galilee near the Mediterranean coast. Micah's concern was that if the Philistines in Gath learned of Israel's predicted destruction, they would laugh with joy at the prospect of the Hebrew nation being punished (2 Samuel 1:20). Instead, the Jews ought to repent of their sins and seek God's forgiveness. They should roll themselves in the dust, the supreme sign of deep sorrow (Jeremiah 6:26; Ezekiel 27:30).

God will not long put up with injustice, but He also will not put up with those who rejoice in the punishment of others. If someone who has hurt you has misfortune, don't be like the people of Gath. Never take joy in the punishment of another. Instead, *"heal the brokenhearted"* (Isaiah 61:1).

GENNESARET

Healthy Faith

As a disciple, Peter had many unusual experiences with Jesus, but none more so than walking on the waters of the Lake of Gennesaret, also called the Sea of Galilee. He did all right until he took his eyes off the Lord and noticed the whitecaps on the water. When Peter began

NAME: "Garden of Riches"
LOCATION: Area NW of Sea of Galilee, p.33
IDENTIFICATION: Both lake and fertile land between Capernaum and Magdala
STORY LINE: Jesus' ministry largely took place on or around Gennesaret
READ IT IN THE BIBLE: Matthew 14:22–36

to sink, Jesus grabbed him and said, *"O you of little faith, why did you doubt?"* (Matthew 14:31).

Jesus and the disciples docked at the plain of Gennesaret, which curves along the western shore of the lake for about four miles between Capernaum and Magdala. The land rises slowly in a westerly direction for about a mile toward the mountains. In Jesus' day, this area was the garden spot of Palestine, and it was where many of His healing miracles took place. One of those miracles was a woman whose faith was in stark contrast to Peter's, who was still wet from his slip in the lake.

A woman who had experienced an irregular menstrual flow for twelve years came to Jesus in faith. She had spent a fortune on doctors, only to find no relief. When she saw Jesus coming she said, *"If only I may touch His clothes I shall be made well"* (Mark 5:28). Not that the Savior's clothes had any power, but her faith did. Imagine how Peter must have felt seeing the healthy faith of this woman after his own failure of faith.

If you have a need today, do you have a healthy faith as well? Remember Jesus' promise: *"If you ask anything in My name, I will do it"* (John 14:14). If God has the will, do you have the faith?

GETHSEMANE

Spiritual Struggle

Are you facing something you know you must do, and yet it's unpleasant and you are dreading it? That's what Jesus experienced in Gethsemane.

The name Gethsemane is used only in Matthew 26:36 and Mark 14:32, although Luke and John also

NAME: "Oil Press"
LOCATION: Immediately E of Jerusalem, p.53
IDENTIFICATION: Olive garden on the west side of the Mount of Olives
STORY LINE: Jesus' prayed here the night before His crucifixion
READ IT IN THE BIBLE: Mark 14:27–50

record Jesus' agony there before His betrayal. Luke says Gethsemane was on *"the Mount of Olives"* (Luke 22:39). John describes it as *"over the Brook Kidron"* (John 18:1). John is the only one to call it a garden.

Jesus had stolen away to this garden before, but never like this time (John 18:1–2). He had prayed before, but never like this time (Matthew 14:23). Jesus had struggled subjecting His deity to His humanity before (Luke 2:51), but never like this time. This time it wasn't just a future event "out there." This time His date with destiny had arrived. Jesus wasn't grappling with whether or not His crucifixion was appropriate. He wasn't debating His Father's will. He was struggling with the fact that what He knew had to be done was only hours away. This wasn't potential anymore. Now it was real. The torture of His passion was at hand. That makes all the more remarkable the stiffness of His resolve: *"Not what I will, but what You will"* (Mark 14:36).

If you're facing something unpleasant today, something you've dreaded for a long time and yet the time has come, draw strength from the heart of Jesus. He faced a spiritual struggle, too, but He knew the Father's will always brings the best result. If He could invite the torture of Calvary, you can invite what you know is right, too.

GILEAD

Promise Keepers

In 1942, General Douglas MacArthur made a famous promise to the people of the Philippines when he was forced to leave the islands. He said, "I shall return." He did.

NAME: "Rugged"

LOCATION: NE of the Jordan River, p.33

IDENTIFICATION: Two and a half of Israel's tribes settled in Gilead

STORY LINE: Reuben, Gad and half the tribe of Manasseh keep their word

READ IT IN THE BIBLE: Numbers 32:1–33; Joshua 22:1–9

It's always an encouragement when people keep their word. Reuben, Gad, and half the tribe of Manasseh encouraged Moses' heart when they kept a promise to him.

The history of Israel is a chronicle of disobedience. God's people were prone to breaking their promises. So you can understand Moses' reticence when two and one half of the tribes wanted to settle outside the

Promised Land in Gilead. But the people of Reuben, Gad, and half the tribe of Manasseh had large herds of cattle and flocks of sheep. The region of Gilead was the high plains east of the Jordan River, between the Yarmuk and Arnon Rivers. It was divided by the Jabbok River. The valleys and hills were well watered by numerous tributaries to these rivers, and it was the perfect place for herds and flocks.

But Moses was concerned these tribes would settle into an agricultural life while Israel still had to fight for every inch of Canaan. Reuben, Gad, and Manasseh vowed that if they were allowed to settle in Gilead, they first would fight until every tribe had received its inheritance. Moses warned them: *"if you do not do so . . . you have sinned against the LORD; and be sure your sin will find you out"* (Numbers 32:23). The tribes kept their word.

Remember that one thing you can give and still keep is your word. Encourage someone today by keeping a promise.

TURQUIE D'ASIE,

ARABIE, PERSE,

CABOUL, BELOUTCHISTAN,

ET TURKESTAN.

Par C. V. Monin.

GREECE

Engaging The World Without Assimilating It

Souvlaki. The Olympics. The Parthenon. Just a few of the things we associate with the country of Greece. Alexander the Great. Socrates. Plato. Just a few people we associate with Greece. But did you know that we

NAME: "The Miry One"
LOCATION: Mediterranean peninsula, p.12
IDENTIFICATION: End of Balkan Peninsula between the Aegean and Ionian Seas
STORY LINE: Country that gave culture to Western civilization
READ IT IN THE BIBLE: Acts 20:1–6

also can thank the Greeks for the flame–thrower, coin–operated machines, and chewing gum?

When you talk about Bible places, you have to talk about Greece. Extending into the Mediterranean from southeastern Europe, Greece consists of northern and central regions connected by a narrow isthmus to a southern peninsula, the Peloponnesus.

The Greeks presented serious challenges both to

pious Jews and early Christians. The Philistines, the perpetual enemies of Israel, originally sailed from the Aegean world to settle in Canaan. The man–centered culture of the Greeks confronted the God–centered culture of Judaism and Christianity. But the early Jews also benefited from trading with the Greeks. And the rapid spread of the Gospel in the first century would have been next to impossible had it not been for widespread knowledge of the Greek language.

The relationship of Jews and Christians to the Greeks helps us better understand how to get along with people whose beliefs are different from our own. We can never allow our faith to be assimilated into the culture, nor can we permit that culture to dictate our beliefs. But we must interact with our culture and recognize that those whose belief systems are different from ours are still people who need the Lord.

Today, don't hide from the culture around you. Engage it. Let your light shine wherever you may be.

HARAN

A Few Days; A Few Decades

W. C. Fields once quipped, "I once spent a year in Philadelphia. I think it was on a Sunday." Sometimes we find ourselves in places where time seems to crawl instead of fly. For Jacob, Haran was not one of those places.

NAME: "Highway"

LOCATION: Northern Mesopotamia, p.13

IDENTIFICATION: Aramean city famous for worship of lunar gods Sin and Nikkal

STORY LINE: Abraham and Jacob lived here while waiting on God

READ IT IN THE BIBLE: Genesis 12:1–9; 27:41–46

A city of northern Mesopotamia, situated on a branch of the Euphrates River, Haran was on the ancient trade route that linked Damascus, Nineveh, and Carchemish. Ezekiel mentions trade between Haran and Tyre (Ezekiel 27:23). When God appeared to Abraham and told him to leave Ur of the Chaldees (Acts 7:2–4), Abraham and his family journeyed as far as Haran, where they lived until the death of his father,

Terah. From here the patriarch moved on to the Land of Promise. But some relatives remained in Haran, and they later became a refuge for Jacob, Abraham's grandson, after he cheated his brother, Esau.

Rebekkah counseled her favorite son, *"Flee to my brother Laban in Haran. And stay with him a few days until your brother's fury turns away"* (Genesis 27:43–44). A few days turned into twenty years. Still, seven of those years were spent acquiring Rachel's hand *"and they seemed but a few days to him because of the love he had for her"* (Genesis 29:20).

If your life has hit a slow spot, ask God to give you something to do, even if it's in a place where you could say, "I spent a week there one night." Don't just kill time, get to know God better by reading His Word. Find someone to tell about His amazing love. Even the most mundane place can become exciting when you invest yourself in something that makes a difference for eternity.

HEBRON

Making Your Death Count

Omaha, Nebraska, police officer Jimmy Wilson, Jr., was initiating a routine traffic stop when the driver stepped out of the vehicle and opened fire, killing him in 1995. The 24–year–old Wilson was an organ donor, and Barbara Fairchild received his heart, adding nine

---

NAME: "Confederacy"
LOCATION: 25 miles SW of Jerusalem, p.33
IDENTIFICATION: Once known as Kiriath–Arba, frequent home of the Patriarchs
STORY LINE: Samson carried the gates of Gaza 38 miles uphill to Hebron
READ IT IN THE BIBLE: Judges 16:23–31

---

unexpected years to her life. Despite the tragedy, Wilson's death had meaning.

Samson was Israel's strongman, but his physical strength was no match for his moral weakness. We all know of his exploits with Delilah, but first he married a Philistine girl from Timnah. Then he visited a prostitute and only escaped Gaza because he tore the city gate from its posts and carried it all the way to Hebron (Judges 16:3). Located at the southern end of the highlands of Jerusalem, Hebron was the burial site of the Patriarchs. David was crowned king of Judah there (2 Samuel 2:1–7). But Hebron was a mountain town (3,300 feet above sea level) whereas Gaza was down near the sea. For Samson to carry the gate uphill more than thirty miles to Hebron was quite a feat.

But Samson's greatest achievement was yet to come. When three thousand Philistines gathered in Gaza at the temple of Dagon, Samson pushed against the support pillars and the roof caved in. *The dead that he killed at his death were more than he had killed in his life* (Judges 16:30).

What will your death mean for others? Perhaps the Gospel preached at your funeral will bring others to Christ. Perhaps through the finances provided by your will, Gospel ministries will be strengthened. Perhaps, like Samson, you will do more damage to the enemy in your death than in your life. Be a good steward in death. It's your final opportunity.

MOUNT HERMON

Mountain Dew from God's Word

Mountain Dew is a soft drink especially popular with teenagers. But mountain dew in the Bible is also a symbol for the blessing of God. If you "do the Dew," your thirst is quenched. If God does the dew, you are refreshed eternally.

NAME: "Sanctuary"
LOCATION: Israel's northern boundary, p.33
IDENTIFICATION: The snow–capped highest peak in the Middle East
STORY LINE: The dew of Mt. Hermon symbolizes the blessing of God
READ IT IN THE BIBLE: Psalm 133; Psalm 89:1–15

Mount Hermon is located at the northern end of the territory conquered by Joshua. It was the upper boundary of the half–tribe of Manasseh and, in general, considered to be the northern boundary of Israel (Deuteronomy 3:8; Joshua 11:17). Hermon towers 9,166 feet over the valley of Lebanon and is about thirteen miles long. On a clear day travelers to northern

Israel have a breathtaking view of the snow–capped Mount Hermon.

But Mount Hermon meant much more to people living in the Holy Land. The writers of the Bible speak of the dew of Hermon as symbolic of the blessings of God *"descending upon the mountains of Zion"* (Psalm 133:3).

Dew is moisture that condenses when the days are warm and the nights are cool. These tiny droplets of water on the ground each morning were an important source of moisture for the people of the ancient Near East. The hot days evaporated much of the region's moisture, and rain was often sparse. Dew was an anticipated, essential blessing from God each morning.

When your life is stressed and strained, your spirit dry and dehydrated, maybe all you need is the dew of God's blessing. Take some time today to read about God's blessings. Psalms 89 and 133 are good places to begin. Read God's Word and find peace where you were parched and serenity where you were stressed.

HINNOM

A Powerful Reminder to Pray

Every civilization produces waste byproducts. Garbage. Trash. Refuse. Rubbish. There's just no nice name for it. And every large city needs a landfill. Jerusalem's was the valley of Hinnom.

NAME: "Lamentation"
LOCATION: Immediately S of Jerusalem, p.53
IDENTIFICATION: Deep ravine where child sacrifices took place
STORY LINE: The valley of Hinnom (Gehenna) came to symbolize hell
READ IT IN THE BIBLE: Jeremiah 7:28–34; Revelation 20:11–15

Hinnom was a deep, narrow ravine on the south side of Jerusalem. Because the city's refuse, including the dead bodies of criminals, was burned there, smoke and a noxious stench constantly rose from the valley. But Hinnom became even more notorious because of the idolatrous practices carried out there. An idol to the Ammonite god Molech was placed in the valley, its hands being red hot, and the children of at least two of

Judah's kings—Ahaz and Manasseh—were made to pass between these hands as they were burned alive in sacrifice (2 Kings 16:3; 21:6; Psalm 106:37). Because this practice was strongly prohibited in the Law (Leviticus 18:21; 20:2–5), it's little wonder Jeremiah referred to Hinnom in symbolizing God's judgment upon His people (Jeremiah 2:23; 7:30–32).

Hinnom's name became synonymous with the place of final punishment for the wicked (Isaiah 66:24). Jesus said it was the final habitat of destruction for the unrepentant wicked (Matthew 10:28). Consequently, the fiery abyss of Gehenna (Mark 9:43) is identified as the lake of fire (Revelation 20:14–15) to which all of Satan's soldiers in the long war against God will one day be consigned (Matthew 23:15, 33), together with Satan and his demons (Revelation 19:20).

The symbolism isn't pretty, but it is powerful. Rubbish. Wickedness. Burning. These describe the character of hell and summon us to pray for our unbelieving family members and friends today. Then, after we've prayed, we must be proactive in telling them of God's love and forgiveness.

ISRAEL

Dry Bones and God's Promises

Remember the old spiritual about "Dem bones, dem bones, dem dry bones"? That song was talking about the Jews' return to the land promised them through Father Abraham. Today that land is known as Israel.

NAME: "Prince with God"
LOCATION: East of Mediterranean Sea, pp.13 & 33
IDENTIFICATION: The Promised Land of the Hebrew nation, the people of God
STORY LINE: Israel is back in her land, the "Hinge of the World"
READ IT IN THE BIBLE: Ezekiel 36–37

Israel is in the news almost daily. The land has always been the focus of mankind. Early maps placed Jerusalem at the center of the world. This narrow strip of land connects three great continents—Africa, Asia, and Europe. Jerusalem is sacred to the world's three great religions—Judaism, Christianity, and Islam. This tiny piece of real estate, bordered by Lebanon, Jordan, Egypt, and the Mediterranean Sea, has been called Canaan, Judea, Israel, the land that flows with milk and honey, and much more.

Three sovereign Jewish states have existed on this land under the Abrahamic Covenant. In Genesis 12:1–3 and 15:1–21, God promised the land to Abraham but cautioned that his descendants would not continuously occupy it. The Jewish people were absent from the Holy Land after the Assyrian and Babylonian captivities, and—after the destruction of Jerusalem in A.D. 70— they were like dry bones scattered across the globe for almost two millennia. But God keeps His promises, and in 1948 the Jewish people returned to establish the modern State of Israel. God reassembled that old skeleton and made those dry bones live again.

Someone has estimated that there are 7,487 promises in the Bible. God plans to keep all the ones He has made. It may take some time, but every promise God has made to you can be trusted. The dry bones waited two thousand years. Your wait won't be that long.

ITALY
Global Friendships

When you think of Italy, what comes to your mind? Romance in Rome? Tuscan villas? Spaghetti and tortellini everywhere? How about friends?

Italy is the boot–shaped peninsula that juts southward from central Europe into the Mediterranean

NAME: "Calf–like"
LOCATION: Southern Europe, p.12
IDENTIFICATION: Boot–shaped peninsula between Tyrrhenian and Adriatic Seas
STORY LINE: Italy's capital ruled the world during the first century
READ IT IN THE BIBLE: Romans 16:1–17

Sea. Amazingly, two major mountain ranges—the Alps, which form the northern border, and the Apennines, which form the backbone of the peninsula—occupy 77 percent of the land.

During the second millennium B.C., each area of the peninsula came to be known by the tribe that inhabited it. Among the most important were the

Latins, who settled in the valley of the Tiber River. According to historian Antiochus of Syracuse (who lived in the fifth century B.C.), around 1300 B.C. King Italos ruled the southwestern part of the peninsula, and eventually the whole country was called "Italy."

The word "Italy" appears in three places in the New Testament. Paul befriended Priscilla and Aquila when Emperor Claudius expelled the Jews from Rome (Acts 18:2). Italy was Paul's destination as a result of his legal appeal to Caesar (Acts 27:1, 6). And the writer of Hebrews sends his readers the greetings of "those from Italy" (Hebrews 13:24).

Paul greeted twenty–seven friends by name in the final chapter of his Roman epistle, even though he had not yet been to Rome at the time. Having Christian friends all over the world encourages us to be world Christians. If you are a bit provincial in your Christian friendships, began praying for believers elsewhere in the world and be open to befriending them.

JABBOK

Welcome Resistance

After cheating his twin brother out of his birthright, Jacob had been on the lam for twenty years. Now it was time to go home. On the journey back to Canaan, his entourage came to the ford of Jabbok. Jacob sent his wives and children over the brook, but he stayed behind.

NAME: "Flowing"
LOCATION: 15 miles N of Dead Sea, p.33
IDENTIFICATION: Strong perennial river flowing westward into the Jordan River
STORY LINE: At the Jabbok, Jacob wrestled with the Angel of God
READ IT IN THE BIBLE: Genesis 32:22–30

He needed time to prepare mentally for the next day when he would face his brother, Esau, for the first time in two decades.

The source of the Jabbok is a spring near Amman, today's capital city of Jordan. From there the Jabbok loops northeast before turning west and slashing a deep canyon until it flows gently into the Jordan River.

Throughout its sixty–mile course, the Jabbok drops an average of eighty feet in elevation each mile.

That night, as Jacob rested near the rushing waters, a man came out of nowhere and challenged him. During the all–night wrestling match neither gained the upper hand, but the mysterious wrestler was able to dislocate Jacob's hip. Jacob refused to give up. He recognized the superiority of his opponent (the Bible calls him an angel of God, Hosea 12:2–5) yet Jacob said, *"I will not let You go unless You bless me!"* (Genesis 32:26).

Jacob was not wrestling with God in a battle of wills. This was a tune–up, a trial heat, a struggle to get Jacob ready and steel his resolve for the next day. Often when we meet God's resistance in our lives it's designed to make us stronger. Jacob became Israel; the cheater became a prince.

Don't complain about God's resistance in your life; welcome it. It may be His way of steeling your resolve to make you a royal.

151

JACOB'S WELL

The Importance of Personal Faith

As a boy, people told me how impressive the Alps were. I had no reason to doubt them, but when I saw those mountains for myself, I truly understood their majesty.

That's the way it was at Jacob's well, a site two miles southeast of modern Nablus. The well is located

NAME: "Flowing"

LOCATION: 30 miles N of Jerusalem, p.33 (Sychar)

IDENTIFICATION: Well on land bought by Jacob between Mt. Ebal and Mt. Gerizim

STORY LINE: Here Jesus introduced a Samaritan woman to eternal water

READ IT IN THE BIBLE: John 4:1–42

between Mount Ebal and Mount Gerizim. The first time I visited there I dropped a stone into the well and discovered that it is about a hundred feet deep. The water is pure, plentiful, and very cold.

One day Jesus and His disciples stopped at the nearby village of Sychar on their way to Galilee. When a Samaritan woman came to draw water from the well,

Jesus asked her for a drink. She was shocked; there was bad blood between Jews and Samaritans. She politely called Him *"Sir"* (John 4:15). Then Jesus told her things about her personal life that He couldn't possibly have known and she called Him *"prophet"* (v. 19). Then the woman rushed into the village and said, *"Come, see a Man who told me all things that I ever did"* and she called him *"Christ"* (v. 29). The men of the village hurried to the well, encountered Jesus for themselves, and said to the woman, *"Now we believe, not because of what you said, for we have heard for ourselves and know that this is indeed the Christ."* They called Him *"Savior"* (v. 42).

Believing what others say about Jesus is one thing; encountering Him personally is something else. Until you meet Jesus personally, you cannot appreciate that He is much more than a teacher or prophet. He is the Savior of the world.

*By faith Abraham
obeyed when he was
called to go out to
the place which he would
receive as an inheritance.*

And he went out,
not knowing
where he was going.

HEBREWS 11:8

VALLEY OF JEHOSHAPHAT

The Valley of Decision

Many places in the Bible evoke images of judgment. The bema seat at Corinth (Acts 18:12–17). The

Name: "Valley where Jehovah Judges"
Location: Immediately E of Jerusalem, p.53
Identification: Known also as the Valley of Decision where Jehovah judges
Story Line: Here Jehovah judges all the nations who mistreated Israel
Read it in the Bible: Joel 3:1–21

judgment hall of Pilate (John 19:13). And the Valley of Jehoshaphat.

Located east of Jerusalem between the Old City and the Mount of Olives, the Valley of Jehoshaphat literally means the "valley where Jehovah judges." It's also called the Kidron Valley, and this small region receives the connotation of a place of judgment from the prophet Joel.

The message of Joel 3, and of a parallel passage in Zechariah 14, is that just like Jehoshaphat defeated his enemies in this valley (2 Chronicles 20:14–30), here God will destroy those who oppose Him. Also, because both Zechariah and Joel mention the Mount of Olives—coupled with the fact that Christ ascended to heaven from this mountain—it's very possible that people in this valley will look up to witness Christ's return (Acts 1:11), when *the kingdoms of this world have become the kingdoms of our Lord and of His Christ, and He shall reign forever and ever!* (Revelation 11:15).

The Valley of Jehoshaphat is often called the "Valley of Decision." Each of us must decide for ourselves whether we will remain at war with God or will accept His peace treaty purchased at Calvary when His Son paid the penalty for our sins (John 3:14–18). You don't have to travel to Jerusalem to make that decision, but to avoid God's judgment, you must decide.

JERICHO

First Victory

In any sporting event, every victory is important, but none like the first. It sets the tone for all the others. When the Israelites entered the Promised Land, they needed a decisive first victory, and they got it.

NAME: "Moon City"
LOCATION: 15 miles NE of Jerusalem, p.33
IDENTIFICATION: One of the world's oldest continuously inhabited cities
STORY LINE: Joshua's victory here gave Israel a foothold in Canaan
READ IT IN THE BIBLE: Joshua 5:13–6:27

Jericho was a military outpost located a few miles west of the Jordan River and just northwest of the Dead Sea. Fed by Elisha's Spring, it was a lush oasis amid dunes of sand. The Old Testament calls it *the city of palm trees* (Deuteronomy 34:3; 2 Chronicles 28:15).

Israel was camped on the east bank of the Jordan when Joshua sent spies on a reconnaissance mission into Jericho. While the spies' report was helpful, the battle plan for conquering Jericho was absolutely divine. In a pre–incarnate appearance as the Captain of the Lord's army, Jesus Christ gave Joshua a battle plan that was unconventional, to say the least. The Israelites would daily march around the city without speaking for six days. On the seventh day, they would circle the fortress seven times, the priests would blast their trumpets, and the walls of Jericho would come tumbling down. It happened just as the Lord said.

That victory was important for Israel. It encouraged them that maybe they could claim the land after all. It was also important for Joshua. Joshua 6:27 says, *"So the LORD was with Joshua, and his fame spread throughout all the country."*

If you're facing difficult challenges today, don't worry about the war; concentrate on winning the first battle. A first victory will provide the encouragement for other battles ahead.

JERUSALEM

Enjoying the Peace Jerusalem Never Knew

Sometimes the hardest hearts belong to the people who have been blessed the most. Jesus wept for the hardhearted people of Jerusalem in His time, and things haven't changed much today.

NAME: "City of Peace"
LOCATION: 12 Miles W of Dead Sea, pp.13, 33 & 53
IDENTIFICATION: City sacred to Judaism, Christianity and Islam; the Holy City
STORY LINE: Jesus wept over the hardness of the city's heart
READ IT IN THE BIBLE: Matthew 23:1–39

Jerusalem is *"the city which the LORD had chosen . . . to put His name there"* (2 Chronicles 12:13). It is *"the holy city"* (Nehemiah 11:1). Zion, city of our God, is *"the joy of the whole earth"* (Psalm 48:2). Like Rome, Jerusalem is set on a cluster of hills 2,500 feet above sea level. The capital of Israel, Jerusalem is located twelve miles west of the Dead Sea and thirty–three miles east of the Mediterranean coast. The earliest mention of

Jerusalem (Urusalimum) is found in the Egyptian Execration Texts, which date from the 19th and 18th centuries before Christ.

Sacred to the world's three great monotheistic religions—Christianity, Judaism, and Islam—Jerusalem means "City of Peace," but it has never lived up to its name. Days before a mob cried, *"Crucify Him, Crucify Him!"* Jesus paused on the western slopes of the Mount of Olives overlooking Jerusalem and lamented, *"O Jerusalem, Jerusalem, the one who kills the prophets and stones those who are sent to her! How often I wanted to gather your children together, as a hen gathers her chicks under her wings, but you were not willing!"* (Matthew 23:37). He wanted to give Jerusalem peace, but they wouldn't accept it.

If you have been cold and indifferent toward Jesus, let Him warm your heart with His love. Enjoy the peace that Jerusalem never found. Enjoy the Savior.

JEZREEL

Living By The Golden Rule

The world is filled with powerful people who think that might makes right. Saddam Hussein waged a war of genocide against the Kurds in northern Iraq. Using mustard gas, he slaughtered as many as 200,000 of his own people—because he could. Many top business

NAME: "God Sows"
LOCATION: 56 miles N of Jerusalem, p.33
IDENTIFICATION: Winter palace of the kings of the Northern Kingdom
STORY LINE: King Ahab took Naboth's vineyard next to the king's palace
READ IT IN THE BIBLE: 1 Kings 21:1–29

executives have been charged with corporate greed, fraud, or insider trading—offenses they committed because they could.

In ancient times, one such person was King Ahab of Israel. In the days of his father, King Omri (885–874 B.C.), Jezreel was chosen as the site of the king's winter capital. The royal palace was adjacent to a vineyard owned by Naboth. When Ahab offered to buy Naboth's vineyard so he could plant a vegetable garden, Naboth refused because it was family land, part of his inheritance. Jezebel, Ahab's wicked queen, hatched a plan to malign Naboth's character and have him killed. As a result, God severely punished the dynasty of Ahab, and Jezebel herself was thrown to the dogs through an upper window (2 Kings 9:30–37).

Historian Lord Acton (1834–1902) said, "Power tends to corrupt and absolute power corrupts absolutely." The 9/11 attacks on the World Trade Center and Pentagon were yet more examples of tyrants doing what they wanted because they could.

We must never allow our attitudes towards others to degenerate to that of political power players or business barons. Jesus said, *"Whatever you want men to do to you, do also to them"* (Matthew 7:12). Ahab and Jezebel learned that lesson too late, but it's not too late for us. The Golden Rule is still the best rule to live by.

JORDAN RIVER

Longing For Heaven

From the days of antiquity, a great geological fault has extended three thousand miles from the mountains of Lebanon to central Mozambique in East Africa. In Israel, this fault is dominated by the Jordan River.

NAME: "Descending"
LOCATION: In Israel's Rift Valley, p.33
IDENTIFICATION: Israel's major river flowing south into the Dead Sea
STORY LINE: River supernaturally stopped so Israel could cross
READ IT IN THE BIBLE: Joshua 3:1–4:24

The Jordan is formed from four streams in northern Galilee and flows south into the Sea of Galilee, 686 feet below sea level. Then it travels a snakelike path 200 miles and descends to more than 1,300 feet below sea level at the Dead Sea.

The Israelites crossed the Jordan River when they entered the Promised Land (Joshua 3:14–17). The Syrian general Naaman bathed in the Jordan and his leprosy was healed (2 Kings 5:8–14). Jesus was baptized by John the Baptist in the Jordan (Matthew 3:13–17). Peter confessed that Jesus was the *"Christ, the Son of the living God"* at Caesarea Philippi, which is at Banias, one of the sources of the Jordan (Matthew 16:13–20).

But the Jordan River also has a symbolic meaning. "Crossing the Jordan" signifies dying, crossing from life's toil to heaven's rest. One hymn says, "On Jordan's stormy banks I stand / And cast a wishful eye / To Canaan's fair and happy land / Where my possessions lie. / I am bound for the promised land / I am bound for the promised land / O, who will come and go with me? I am bound for the promised land."

There comes a time when we all must stand at Jordan's stormy banks. Make sure you live life now so that your greatest treasures are not left behind but are waiting to meet you in Canaan's fair and happy land.

KADESH BARNEA

Robbed By Fear

When needy miners in British Columbia decided to strip the abandoned Fort Alcan of everything useable, they discovered that the prison walls were nothing but wallboard, made of clay and paper, only painted to resemble iron. But the semblance of iron was so

NAME: "Holy"

LOCATION: On southern edge of Canaan, pp.13 & 33

IDENTIFICATION: Home to the Israelites for 38 years because of disobedience

STORY LINE: Ten spies were afraid to enter the land; two were confident

READ IT IN THE BIBLE: Numbers 13:1–14:24

convincing that no prisoner ever tried to escape from the Fort Alcan prison. Fear had kept them from freedom. Often the blessing of God is also missed or delayed because of fear. Kadesh Barnea was a place of missed blessing for Israel.

When God delivered Israel from slavery in Egypt, He led them on an adventure across the sands of Sinai to the Promised Land. But that adventure became a forty–year fiasco. Kadesh Barnea was an oasis on the northern edge of Sinai, just south of Canaan. From there Moses sent spies into Canaan on a reconnaissance mission, but only Joshua and Caleb came back with positive reports. The rest surrendered to fear when they saw the giants in the land.

Life is filled with challenges and with giants. But it is also filled with the promises of God to defeat those giants. Deuteronomy 20:1 promises, *"When you go out to battle against your enemies, and see horses and chariots and people more numerous than you, do not be afraid of them; for the LORD your God is with you."* Hebrews 13:5 promises, *"I will never leave you nor forsake you."*

Don't let your fears rob you of God's victories. Remember, He is with you every step of the way. Draw strength from His presence and live as a victor, not a victim.

KIDRON

A Poignant Reminder

The Kidron is both a valley and a stream that lie below the southeast wall of Jerusalem. Both separate the city from the Mount of Olives. Kidron means "gloomy" or "dark," and almost every recorded event that occurred there carries that connotation. For example, when

NAME: "Gloomy"
LOCATION: Immediately E of Jerusalem, p.53
IDENTIFICATION: Valley and stream between Jerusalem and Mt. of Olives
STORY LINE: Jesus crossed this valley on the eve of His betrayal
READ IT IN THE BIBLE: John 18:1–14

Absalom usurped his father's throne, David used the Kidron valley as an escape route to the desert. The people wept bitterly (2 Samuel 15:30) because David was abandoning Jerusalem without a fight.

But the gloomiest night in the Kidron was the night Jesus was betrayed. Above the Kidron Valley sat the Temple. At Passover more than 250,000 lambs were slain for the sacrifices of the people. The blood flowed from under the Temple down the side of the hill to the Kidron Valley, staining the hillside black. It must have been a horrendous sight.

When Jesus made His way from the Upper Room to the Garden of Gethsemane on His final Passover, the blood was already rushing into the Kidron. As the Lord crossed the brook He saw the Kidron running red with the fresh blood of abundant sacrifices. What a poignant reminder that His blood soon would be poured out in a similar sacrifice for all of us.

Take some time to ponder the meaning of the Kidron. If you haven't thanked Jesus lately for dying for you, the Kidron Valley is a wonderful reminder to do so.

"And can it be that I should gain an interest in the Savior's blood? Died He for me, who caused His pain? For me, who Him to death pursued? Amazing love!"

— CHARLES WESLEY

KING'S HIGHWAY

Do Good When You Can

Think of the famous roads in the world. There's the "Silk Road" running 4,000 miles from China, Pakistan, and India through Iran, Iraq, Turkey, and on to Rome. And the Appian Way, the oldest and most celebrated highway of the Roman Empire, extending 350 miles

NAME: "King's Highway"
LOCATION: The Transjordan Plateau, pp.13 & 33
IDENTIFICATION: Highway connecting Damascus with southern Arabia
STORY LINE: Israel's requests were rebuffed by Sihon and Og
READ IT IN THE BIBLE: Numbers 21:21–35

from Rome to Brindisi. And don't forget about the German autobahn system, the M1 in Great Britain, or Interstate 95 in the USA. Major roads have always played a strategic role both in commerce and the passage of people.

One of antiquity's most famous roads became infamous for who was denied the right to travel on it.

The King's Highway ran about 350 miles north and south across the Transjordan plateau, connecting Damascus with the caravan route to southern Arabia (1 Kings 10:2; Ezekiel 27:22). But when Moses and the Israelites wished to use this international highway to travel from Sinai to the Promised Land, they were refused passage through Edom (Numbers 20:17) and the Amorite kingdom of Heshbon (Numbers 21:22). As a result, Israel later defeated these kingdoms for their stubborn refusal of a simple courtesy.

How true ring the words of Proverbs 3:27: *"Do not withhold good . . . when it is in the power of your hand to do so."*

Is there some good you can do someone today without expectation of reward? If so, do it. It's your privilege and it may be their salvation.

LAODICEA

What Makes You Rich?

Ernest Hemingway said, "I live in a vacuum that is as lonely as a radio tube when the batteries are dead, and there is no current to plug into." Hemingway was rich in talent but poor in things that mattered most.

NAME: "Justice of the People"
LOCATION: 95 miles E of Ephesus, p.12
IDENTIFICATION: Largest of three cities on Turkish trade routes to Antioch
STORY LINE: Lukewarm Christians were censured by God
READ IT IN THE BIBLE: Revelation 3:14–22

Laodicea was like that. The largest of three cities lying in a broad valley of central Turkey, Laodicea was like a truck stop on the great highway crossing Asia Minor.

Under the Romans, the city achieved significant commercial importance and became wealthy for three reasons. First, Laodicea became a center for banking and finance. Cicero is known to have cashed bank drafts there in 51 B.C. In addition, the area was famous for raising long-haired sheep with glossy black wool. The wool generated a prosperous textile industry centered both in Colosse and Laodicea. Finally, Laodicea had a famous medical school that developed a popular Phrygian eye powder. When mixed with the dried mud of the nearby Hierapolis thermal springs, it became an effective remedy for eye inflammation and was sold throughout the ancient world.

How appropriate, then, is the warning Jesus gave to the church at Laodicea in Revelation 3:17–18. They thought they were rich, but their prosperity caused them to become tepid about their Christian responsibilities. The church became lukewarm and eternally ineffective.

The Church of the 21st century faces a similar challenge. Today's Church is rich in the things of the world, but often is lukewarm in the things of God. Pray for your church, your pastor, and yourself to keep an eternal perspective on all you do. Don't allow the riches of this life to rob you of the rewards of the next.

LEBANON

What Kind of Tree Are You?

Many places in the world are readily identified by their trees. California has its giant redwoods. The quintessential tree of Great Britain is the oak. And when you mention Lebanon, one tree comes to mind—the cedar.

NAME: "White"
LOCATION: N of Israel, pp. 13 & 33
IDENTIFICATION: Home to the 100–mile–long Lebanon Mountain range
STORY LINE: The cedars of Lebanon were symbols of majesty and pride
READ IT IN THE BIBLE: 1 Kings 5:1–10; Psalm 104

The Lebanon mountain range, the highest peak of which is Mount Hermon, runs about 100 miles before it trails off to the south, becoming the hills of northern Galilee. The high peaks of the range trap the rains moving inland from the Mediterranean Sea and provide copious rainfall, both for the dual strands of the mountain range and the Beqa'a Valley that lies between them. In ancient times, Lebanon was famous for its rich forests. The coastal areas, the Beqa'a Valley, and the lower slopes of the mountains were good for olive trees, fruit trees, and vineyards, but the stately cedar was king. No place could grow a cedar like Lebanon.

In biblical poetry the tall cedars of Lebanon were a symbol of majesty and strength (Judges 9:15; 2 Kings 14:9; Psalms 92:12; 104:16; Isaiah 35:2; 60:13). But they were also a symbol of pride that would eventually fall under the judgment of God (Psalm 29:5; Isaiah 2:13; 10:34; Jeremiah 22:6).

If you were to liken yourself to a tree, what tree would it be? Would you be the fruitful olive that has little stature or strength but is very productive for the good of others? Or would you be like the tall cedar of Lebanon, strong yet proud? Rather than aspire to be something you may regret, ask God to make you the kind of tree He can be proud of (Isaiah 61:3).

LO DEBAR

Lame, But Loved

Facing arrest for being an Anabaptist, Dirck Willems fled for his life across a frozen lake. But when his pursuer broke through the ice, Willems gave up his chance to escape in order to rescue his persecutor. He was then captured, imprisoned, and burned at the stake in 1569.

NAME: "Barren" or "No Pasture"
LOCATION: 7 miles SE of Sea of Galilee, p.33
IDENTIFICATION: A Gadite town east of the Jordan River, near Sea of Galilee
STORY LINE: Lo Debar is where Mephibosheth was living
READ IT IN THE BIBLE: 2 Samuel 9:1–13

Still, one of the greatest feelings in life is to show kindness to someone who cannot, or will not, return it to you. David knew that feeling.

King Saul was jealous of young David and repeatedly tried to kill him. Yet David respected Saul as the anointed of God. When Saul was killed on Mount Gilboa and David became king, he wanted to show kindness to Saul's family because of his friendship with Jonathan, Saul's son. The only relation left was Jonathan's son, Mephibosheth.

When David found Mephibosheth he was living in Lo Debar, which is also called Debir, a Gadite city east of the Jordan River (Joshua 13:26). This was an appropriate place for Saul's grandson, because Lo Debar means "no pasture" or "barren" and Mephibosheth's life was certainly barren. He was separated from the king both by distance and circumstance. He was lame, helpless, and hopeless. But David brought Mephibosheth to his palace with all the privileges of a family member.

In many ways, Mephibosheth is just like you and me. We are separated from God, helpless and hopeless. But God graciously invites us to sit at His table forever. Like Mephibosheth, we are still lame, but the fine cloth of Christ's righteousness now covers our infirmities and we are treated as the King's children. Be grateful for God's grace.

LYSTRA

A Case of Mistaken Identity

Jane Thurgood–Dove was chased down and shot in front of her children. The crime baffled everyone until police began working on the theory that it was a tragic case of mistaken identity. Apparently it was.

NAME: "Ransoming"
LOCATION: Central Turkey, p.13
IDENTIFICATION: Important town near Iconium and Derbe, visited by Paul
STORY LINE: Paul and Barnabas were mistaken for Zeus and Hermes here
READ IT IN THE BIBLE: Acts 14:1–20

The greatest case of mistaken identity in the Bible came when Paul and Barnabas visited Lystra on their first missionary journey. Lystra was located in Lycaonia, the province of interior Asia Minor. Lystra and its sister city, Derbe, were the main population centers in this largely grazing ground for sheep and goats. The town primarily was inhabited by a provincial Anatolian tribe who spoke their own dialect. They were an uneducated people who worshipped the Greek deities Zeus and Hermes, as archaeological evidence attests.

While Paul and Barnabas were preaching the Gospel, they encountered opposition at Iconium and so fled to Lystra and Derbe (Acts 14:6). While there, Paul healed a crippled man who had never walked. Stunned, the locals began to shout that Paul and Barnabus were gods who had come to walk among them. They mistakenly identified Barnabas as Zeus and Paul as Hermes (called by the Latin names "Jupiter" or "Mercury" in some English translations).

With so much concern these days about mistaken identifies, it's good to know who you really are. If you have come to Jesus Christ in faith, you are an heir of God and a co–heir with Jesus Christ (Romans 8:16–17). Being a child of God is the greatest identity you can have. Rejoice in it.

MACHPELAH

Facing Death Confidently

It's strange how little–known places become burial grounds for clusters of important people. For example, Bunhill Fields in London was a cemetery for dissenters. But perhaps the most important cluster burial site was a small cave called Machpelah.

NAME: "Double"
LOCATION: 25 miles SW of Jerusalem, p.33
IDENTIFICATION: Field of trees and cave in the area of Mamre near Hebron
STORY LINE: Abraham purchased a cave in which to bury his wife Sarah
READ IT IN THE BIBLE: Genesis 23:1–20

Located at the end of a field of trees, Abraham purchased this cave from Ephron, a Hittite. The selling price was 400 shekels of silver (Genesis 23:8–19) but money was no object. Abraham bought the cave to provide a proper burial for Sarah, the woman he had loved deeply for more than sixty years. Later, Abraham himself, Isaac his son, Rebekah his daughter–in–law, and Jacob his grandson also would be buried in Machpelah. It became a patriarchal holy ground.

The details relating to Abraham's purchase at Machpelah, when compared with Hittite laws, confirm the historical trustworthiness of the biblical account. Abraham made the transaction in public, before many witnesses. It was done at the city gate where all business transactions occurred. Abraham weighed the silver according to the agreed upon price.

Abraham and Sarah were laid to rest at Machpelah where they await *"the city which has foundations, whose builder and maker is God"* (Hebrews 11:10). They never knew the promises you and I know—promises of resurrection, heaven, the return of the Lord—but they trusted God anyway and embraced His promises *"as strangers and pilgrims on the earth"* (Hebrews 11:13). To face death confidently, we must exercise the faith of Abraham.

MAGDALA

God Loves Dedicated People

"Give me your tired, your poor, your huddled masses yearning to be free . . ." Those words by Emma Lazaras are written on a plaque greeting immigrants at the Statue of Liberty. They speak of the eternal search for freedom from oppression and abuse. But they just as

NAME: "Tower"
LOCATION: W of Sea of Galilee, p.33
IDENTIFICATION: Also called Magadan, small village north of Tiberias
STORY LINE: Home of Mary who was first to meet the resurrected Christ
READ IT IN THE BIBLE: John 19:25–20:18

easily may have been spoken by Jesus of Nazareth to everyone who came to Him seeking freedom from demons and disease.

One of those people was a woman named Mary from the small village of Magdala on the western shore of the Sea of Galilee between Tiberias and Capernaum. Also called Magadan (Matthew 15:39) and

Dalmanutha (Mark 8:10), those who hailed from this tiny town were called Magdalenes.

Mary Magdalene met Jesus when He cast seven demons out of her. She then joined the band of disciples and followed Jesus everywhere (Luke 8:2). Mary was one of the most dedicated friends Jesus had. She was at the foot of the cross when all the male disciples had fled (Mark 15:40; John 19:25). She was there for Jesus' burial (Mark 15:47). She was among the women who first saw the empty tomb (Matthew 28:1; Mark 16:1; and Luke 24:10). Mary was the first person to see Jesus alive after His resurrection (John 20:11–18). In fact, it was Mary who reported to the disciples that we do not serve a dead Savior; we serve a risen Lord. Hallelujah!

You may feel like you are not at the top of the pecking order in your circle of Christian friends, but love the Lord with all your heart and wait and see what He has in store for you. That's what Mary did. It worked for her.

MALTA

You're in Good Hands With God

Sailing into Malta is like sailing into the 19th century. Massive fortifications and cannon emplacements are seen on both sides of the harbor. Out of place in today's world of war by terror, it would have been out of place in Paul's simpler day too.

NAME: "Refuge"
LOCATION: 160 miles S of Italy, p.12
IDENTIFICATION: Island south of Sicily, mentioned only once in the Bible
STORY LINE: Paul washed ashore after shipwrecked on the way to Rome
READ IT IN THE BIBLE: Acts 27:13–28:10

The island of Malta is about sixty miles due south of Sicily. Although largely agricultural, the soil is chalky and the yield is poor. The island has no rivers and is dependent on rainfall and springs for its fresh water.

Only mentioned once in the Bible (Acts 28:1), Malta is famous as the island that rescued Paul. The apostle was sailing from Caesarea to Rome, and storms are frequent on the Mediterranean Sea in winter. Caught by a severe storm and driven helplessly by the wind for two weeks, Paul's ship ran aground on Malta's shore and was broken into pieces by the high surf. Miraculously, all 276 people on board managed to reach the shore alive. Paul was safe, but his troubles weren't over. While putting wood on a fire, he was bitten by a snake. The Maltese natives assumed he was a criminal and this was God's punishment. But when Paul did not die, they did an about face and presumed he was a god (Acts 28:6).

Malta is just a 95–square–mile speck in the Mediterranean Sea, but God had miraculously directed Paul's ship to the safety of its shores. This reminds us that not even the depths of the sea can *"separate us from the love of God which is in Christ Jesus our Lord"* (Romans 8:39). When you are in God's hands, you are in good hands.

MEDEBA

The Center of the World

The prophet Ezekiel described God's people as those gathered from the nations who *"dwell in the midst of the land"* (38:12). Literally, in Hebrew, this phrase is Tabor Ha–aretz and means "the center of the world." In 1581, Heinrich Bunting made a woodcut map

NAME: "Waters of Quiet"
LOCATION: 25 miles S of Amman, p.33
IDENTIFICATION: Here Israel defeated Sihon, king of the Amorites
STORY LINE: Sixth century A.D. mosaic map discovered in 1890 excavations
READ IT IN THE BIBLE: Numbers 21:21–32

depicting the world with Jerusalem dead center, connecting everything else.

One of the most interesting maps of Jerusalem is the Medeba Map. Uncovered in excavations in 1890, this is a mosaic map of Jerusalem dating from the sixth century A.D. It is located in the Jordanian town of Madaba, about six miles south of Hesbon. Madaba, or Medeba, was a Moabite town nestled in the fertile plain northeast of the Dead Sea, about twenty–five miles south of ancient Philadelphia in modern Amman.

Medeba is an important site in its own right. The Amorites defeated Moab here (Numbers 21:30). Israel defeated Sihon, king of the Amorites, at Medeba and the town was assigned to Reuben's tribe (Joshua 13:9, 16). It was at Medeba that David routed an Aramean army hired by the Ammonites to attack his forces (1 Chronicles 19:7). According to the Moabite Stone, an ancient monument discovered in 1868, the town was once controlled by Omri and Ahab of Israel, and King Mesha rebuilt Medeba in the eighth century B.C.

But Medeba is best known for its map of Jerusalem, a city whose importance can never be understated. *"Yet I have chosen Jerusalem, that My name may be there,"* said Jehovah (2 Chronicles 6:6). Only Jerusalem is called *"the Holy City"* (Nehemiah 11:1; Isaiah 52:1). Pray for the peace of Jerusalem (Psalm 122:6). When the center of the world has peace, the world will have peace.

MEGIDDO

Real Proximity

In Olney, England, a certain fence separates two backyards. One neighbor was William Cowper, author of the hymn "God Moves in a Mysterious Way." The other neighbor was John Newton, who wrote "Amazing Grace." That's proximity.

NAME: "Place of Troops"
LOCATION: 56 miles N of Jerusalem, pp.13 & 33
IDENTIFICATION: City, plain and valley at SE edge of the plain of Esdraelon
STORY LINE: Battle of Armageddon will be fought on this plain
READ IT IN THE BIBLE: Revelation 16:1–21

The Bible records an even more amazing story of proximity. The city of Megiddo overlooked the southwestern edge of the plain of Esdraelon on the main route between Mesopotamia and Egypt. Its strategic position made Megiddo one of the most important military fortifications in the Holy Land.

The valley it guarded has witnessed some of the

"He is not here;
for *He is risen*,
as He said.
Come, see the place
where the Lord lay."

MATTHEW 28:6

MOAB

How to Defeat Temptation

Snickerdoodles, those delightful cookies sprinkled with cinnamon and sugar, are my downfall. I can pass up a chocolate chip cookie, a sugar cookie, even a fortune cookie, but I have trouble resisting a snickerdoodle.

NAME: "Of My Father"
LOCATION: E of the Dead Sea, pp.13 & 33
IDENTIFICATION: Kingdom measuring 20 by 60 miles on the Transjordan plateau
STORY LINE: Israel sinned in worshiping Moab's national god, Chemosh
READ IT IN THE BIBLE: 1 Kings 11:1–13

For Israel, Moab was a tempting snickerdoodle. Situated on the high plateau east of the Dead Sea, Moab was a small kingdom. At the height of its power, it encompassed only about sixty miles north to south and twenty miles east to west. Still, the Moabites and their religion had a significantly adverse effect on Israel.

King Balak of Moab fought against Israel and hired Balaam to pronounce a curse on them (Numbers 22–24).

The Moabite king Eglon oppressed the Jews until he was assassinated by Ehud (Judges 3:12–30). During the reigns of Saul and David, Moab and Israel were at war almost constantly. In fact, conflict between Moab and her neighbors did not stop until King Nebuchadnezzar destroyed the Moabite kingdom in the sixth century B.C. (Ezekiel 25:8–11). It was Solomon, however, who failed most miserably to keep Moabite influence out of Israel. Solomon brought Moabite women into his harem, and they brought with them their chief god, Chemosh. Solomon built a high place for Chemosh (1 Kings 11:1, 7) and Israel began a spiritually adulterous relationship with the Moabite god.

Israel never learned how to handle temptation. Your number one weapon to defeat temptation is to avoid it (2 Timothy 2:22). Solomon never learned that. Stay away from that person or thing that gets to you. Temptation is best defeated by not engaging it. That's not the coward's way out; that's the winner's way out. Vigilance is the price of both liberty and purity.

MOUNT MORIAH

Trusting or Arguing

Adoniram Judson was a pioneer missionary to Burma, now called Myanmar. While serving Christ there, Judson lost two wives and five of his children. His life was a long series of setbacks and sacrifices, but he never argued with God or lost faith in Him. He wrote, "If I

Name: "Jehovah Provides"
Location: East side of Jerusalem, p.53
Identification: Land and mountain where Solomon's Temple eventually was built
Story Line: Abraham took Isaac to sacrifice him on this mountain
Read it in the Bible: Genesis 22:1–19

had not felt certain that every additional trial was ordered by infinite love and mercy, I could not have survived my accumulated sufferings."

Abraham understood this. In Genesis 22, God told the patriarch, *"Take now your son, your only son Isaac, whom you love, and go to the land of Moriah, and offer him there as a burnt offering on one of the mountains of which I shall tell you"* (v. 2). There were so many things that Abraham could not understand about God's command. Isaac was the promised child for whom Sarah and he had awaited so many years. Why would God want the old patriarch to sacrifice him? But Abraham's faith outdistanced his bewilderment, and he made the three–day journey to the land of Moriah without argument. When Isaac innocently questioned where the lamb was for the sacrifice, Abraham confidently asserted, *"My son, God will provide for Himself the lamb for the burnt offering"* (v. 8). How did he know that was true?

The truth is, everything Abraham did was not because he knew, but because he trusted. He didn't know what would happen, but he believed God and that's all that mattered.

You may not fully understand what's happening in your life, but trusting God is always more fruitful than arguing with Him. Blessing comes from trusting. Be blessed.

NAZARETH

Having a Heart for Your Hometown

Recently I was driving across the country when I got off the interstate to see Winterset, Iowa. Winterset is a quaint village with covered bridges and modest homes. One of them, a four-room house on Court Street, was the birthplace of Marion Morrison, better known as John Wayne.

NAME: "Watchtower"
LOCATION: 70 miles N of Jerusalem, p.33
IDENTIFICATION: Small mountain village north of the Plain of Esdraelon
STORY LINE: Jesus was rejected by family and friends in His hometown
READ IT IN THE BIBLE: Luke 4:13–30

Nazareth was like that—so small and isolated that it is not even mentioned in the Old Testament, the Apocrypha, the Jewish writings, or the histories of Josephus. Situated about fifteen miles west of the Sea of Galilee and twenty miles east of the Mediterranean, Nazareth wasn't on any main road. It was home to poor farmers and at least one carpenter. Hardly anyone would know of the town had not that carpenter's wife given birth to Jesus, the Messiah of Israel and Savior of the world.

Sometime after Jesus was born in Bethlehem, Mary and Joseph returned to Nazareth (Matthew 2:23). Jesus grew up there (Luke 2:39–40, 51), leaving the village when He began His earthly ministry. Although Jesus was often identified as *"Jesus of Nazareth"* (John 18:5, 7), the New Testament records only one subsequent visit by Jesus to His boyhood home. On this occasion, Jesus preached in the synagogue and was rejected by His own townspeople.

If your hometown is not known for anything else, let it be known for someone who cared enough to tell friends and family that judgment awaits them, but God loves them, and Jesus died for them. They may not believe, like the people of the tiny village of Nazareth, but they need to hear. Reach out to the world, but don't forget your hometown.

MOUNT NEBO

Mitigating Grace

Chuck Colson was President Richard Nixon's right-hand man. When the scandal over Watergate broke, he was one of those convicted and sentenced to prison. But while incarcerated, Colson came to faith in

Name: "Elevation"
Location: E of the Jordan River, p.33
Identification: High mountain opposite the plains of Jericho
Story Line: From Mount Nebo Moses viewed the Promised Land
Read it in the Bible: Deuteronomy 34:1–5

Christ as Savior and experienced God's mercy mingled with grace.

Moses also experienced God's mercy mingled with grace. The distinguished leader of the Jews had his hands full. On their journey from Egyptian bondage the people grumbled about everything possible.

In the Wilderness of Zin the Israelites were without water but not without complaint. God told Moses to take Aaron's rod, stand before a rock, and speak to the rock. Fresh water would gush forth. But the faith of the frustrated Moses faltered, and instead he hastily struck the rock twice. This tragic disobedience kept Moses from entering the Promised Land.

Later, when Israel came to the mountains of Moab, Moses stood on the high peak of Nebo, which is also called Pisgah. From this vantage point just east of the northern end of the Dead Sea, God permitted Moses to view the Promised Land even though he would never enter it. This moment of grace is so much like God. Unbelief kept Moses from the full blessing, but divine grace gave him a piece of it.

When you're experiencing God's displeasure because of your sin, look for His grace as well. Even when sin and unbelief keep you from intimate fellowship with your Father, His grace can still offer you an opportunity to come close.

NEGEV

Victories and Defeats

Perhaps the most intriguing, foreboding area of the Holy Land is the Negev. Evoking images of *Lawrence of Arabia,* the Negev is the southernmost region of Palestine. The root word means "to be dry or parched" and nowhere is that more likely than in the Negev.

NAME: "South" or "Dry"

LOCATION: Southern region of Israel, pp.13 & 33

IDENTIFICATION: The parched land between Beersheba and Kadesh Barnea

STORY LINE: Israel's divine claim to the Promised Land included the Negev

READ IT IN THE BIBLE: Numbers 34:1–12; Deuteronomy 34:1–12

An area with no clearly defined geographical boundaries, the Negev stretches from Beersheba to Kadesh Barnea and from the Mediterranean Sea to the Arabah more than seventy miles away.

When Moses reached the end of his days, God led him to the top of Mount Nebo in Jordan, opposite the northern end of the Dead Sea. From here the Lord showed him the land of Gilead to the north. On the horizon were the distant hills of Naphtali, Ephraim, and Manasseh. Directly opposite was the land of Judah and beyond that the Mediterranean. To the south lay the dusty Negev and immediately below him the Valley of Jericho. No supernatural eyesight was needed by Moses to see all this territory; his eyes had not dimmed with old age. From Nebo, on a clear day, glimpses of all this land can be seen. Moses could see it all, but he would never enjoy any of it because of his failure to obey God (Numbers 20).

The Negev was the scene of Moses' greatest victories and greatest defeats. It left an indelible imprint on him. What imprint will your victories and defeats leave on you? Will faithfulness bring you God's blessing or will frustration withhold it from you? Make sure that when God asks you to speak to your rock you don't beat it in frustration. His way is always the best way.

NILE

God Will Not Share His Glory

"I am the LORD" is an expression used 163 times in the Old Testament to remind us there is only one God. *"I am the LORD, that is My name; and My glory I will not give to another"* (Isaiah 42:8). God will not share His glory with another god or any of His creation.

NAME: "River"
LOCATION: Egypt and Sudan, p.13
IDENTIFICATION: At 4,160 miles, the Nile is the world's longest river
STORY LINE: Like no other river, the Nile influenced its nations
READ IT IN THE BIBLE: Genesis 41:1–32; Exodus 7:14–8:15

The Nile was God's creation. More than any other river, the Nile influenced the nation along its banks. Without the Nile, Egypt never would have become a world power. The Greek historian Herodotus called Egypt the "gift of the Nile." The Nile's annual flooding fertilized the land with silt and new organic materials, making it exceptionally productive.

So important was the Nile to the Egyptians that they worshipped it in the form of the god Hapi, which was always depicted as a male figure with a somewhat rotund body, representing the abundance brought to the Egyptians by the Nile. Little wonder, then, in Pharaoh's dream, the seven lean and seven fat cows arose out of the Nile (Genesis 41:18–19). It was the source of life for Egypt. And when the plagues destroyed the power of Egypt, many of them involved the Nile. Imagine how crushing it was for the Egyptians to see their deified river turn to blood before their eyes.

God will not allow people or places to cheat Him of the affection that belongs to God alone. Even what is good can become evil to us if we love it more than we love God. Investigate your own life and make sure nothing has escaped the altar upon which you lay everything before God.

NINEVEH

Love Your Enemy

Have you ever been asked to do something good for someone you disliked? How about someone you outright hated? Jonah was an eighth century B.C. prophet called by God to preach repentance to his hated enemies the Ninevites. No other prophet was so

Name: "Abode of Ninus"
Location: Northern Iraq, p.13
Identification: Assyria's capital, one of the great cities of the world
Story Line: Jonah was called by God to preach repentance in Nineveh
Read it in the Bible: Jonah 1:1–4:11

strongly Jewish (see Jonah 1:9), yet none other was so completely directed to minister to a non–Jewish nation.

Nineveh was one of the capitals of the Assyrian Empire. Located in northern Iraq near Mosul, the brick wall that surrounded Nineveh was eight miles long with fifteen gates guarded by colossal stone bulls. Jonah described Nineveh as so large it took three days just to cross or circumnavigate it (Jonah 3:3). Six books of the Old Testament refer to Nineveh (Genesis, 2 Kings, Isaiah, Nahum, Zephaniah and Jonah). The tribute paid by Israel's King Menahem (2 Kings 15:19–20) and the spoil taken at the fall of Samaria (Isaiah 8:4) were brought to Nineveh. Here Sennacherib received tribute from Hezekiah king of Judah (2 Kings 18:14–16). Nahum declared the final downfall of the city in vivid language, as did Zephaniah (Zephaniah 2:13–15). Nineveh was destroyed by a coalition of Babylonians, Medes, and Scythians in 612 B.C.

Jonah knew the kindly character of God, and he didn't want to share that kindness with the people of Ninevah (Jonah 4:2).

It's good news that God is gracious, merciful, and slow to anger—even toward those we don't like. Never begrudge God's mercy to someone who needs it, even if that person has been a problem to you. If God can forgive them, shouldn't you?

MOUNT OF OLIVES

Where Heaven and Earth Meet

It's where heaven meets earth. It's the connection between two worlds. It's the heights of the Mount of Olives.

This prominent ridge just east of Jerusalem is capped by three summits. The northernmost is Mount Scopus, where the Crusaders got their first glimpse of

NAME: "Mount of Olives"
LOCATION: Immediately E of Jerusalem, pp.33 & 53
IDENTIFICATION: North–South ridge of Judean mountains above Kidron Valley
STORY LINE: Jesus ascended to the Father from the Mount of Olives
READ IT IN THE BIBLE: Acts 1:1–11

the Holy City. The southernmost is called the "Mount of Offense" because it was here Solomon built temples for his foreign wives. The central peak, which rises to 2,684 feet, is the traditional Mount of Olives.

David fled from Absalom over the Mount of Olives (2 Samuel 15:30). Jesus began His triumphal entry into Jerusalem from here (Mark 11). During His passion week, Jesus taught on the Mount of Olives (Mark 13), spent His evenings there (Luke 21:37), and from a garden there was arrested and led to His crucifixion. (Mark 14:32).

But the primary importance of the Mount of Olives is that it is the touch point between heaven and earth. Forty days after His resurrection Jesus ascended to His Father from the top of this mountain (Acts 1:1–11). And in his apocalyptic vision, the prophet Zechariah declares that at the final judgment the Lord's *"feet will stand on the Mount of Olives . . . And the Mount of Olives shall be split in two, from east to west, making a very large valley"* (Zechariah 14:4). It was from here Jesus went up, and to here He will come down again.

No real estate on earth more clearly demonstrates that it is Jesus who connects us to the Father (1 Timothy 2:5). Nobody can take us up to the God of heaven but Jesus, and nobody brings God's heaven down to us like Him.

O N O

Staying On Mission

It's been observed that basically there are two kinds of people in the world: those who lead, and those who read books on leadership. Nehemiah was of the first kind.

In 539 B.C., Persian King Cyrus decreed that the Jews could return to their homeland; Zerubbabel led

> NAME: "Grief"
> LOCATION: 30 miles NW of Jerusalem, p.33
> IDENTIFICATION: A plain, valley or Benjamite town built by Shemed
> STORY LINE: Nehemiah would not stop God's work for talks with adversaries
> READ IT IN THE BIBLE: Nehemiah 6:1–13

almost fifty thousand of them in the first emigration back to the Holy Land in 538 B.C. (Ezra 2). Ezra led the second wave of four thousand Jews 119 years later (Ezra 7–8). The year was 458 B.C. Fourteen years later, Nehemiah led the third wave. The year was 444 B.C.

Nehemiah set about to rebuild the wall of Jerusalem, but he faced stiff opposition, mainly from Sanballat the

Horonite, Tobiah the Ammonite, and Geshum the Arab. Because they could not defeat Nehemiah in open battle, this trio of evil tried to trick him into meeting with them in the plain of Ono. Ono was a Benjamite town built by Shemed (1 Chronicles 8:12) seven miles southeast of Joppa on the Mediterranean coast of Israel.

But Nehemiah saw through their scheme to ambush and kill him. When his enemies invited him for a conference to the plain of Ono, Nehemiah said, "Oh no!" His reason: *I am doing a great work, so that I cannot come down. Why should the work cease while I leave it and go down to you?* (Nehemiah 6:3).

Are you doing a great work for God? Maybe you're raising godly children or serving on the missions committee at church. Whatever you are doing for God, don't let the enemy sidetrack you. No consultation with your enemies is ever more important than simply keeping at God's work.

DIMIDIA TRIBVS MANASSE
hoc est, ea Terræ Sanctæ pars, quam Manaßæ
dimidia tribus in regionis diuisione obtinuit.

Miliaria vnius horæ.

PARS

Galaad mons. 50

Rabba

rcus Basan . 24

50

Pella 74

Camon. 28

Casphor. 32

Galaad 52

SAN.

Terra Galaad. 51

Carnaim

30

Arbel 14

Arx

io Ga litica

53

Basan 99

Ragaba . 79

23

Abela . 3

Nemus Iabes 72

Carnion 31

Gamala

Iabes Galaad 61

Arga. 3

GAN.

TUM.

ANASSE.

Gergesei. 55

Regio Gera lenorum

Gadara 49

Amathus. 9

77

Via

Cepharno ma. 36

Enganna 47

55

Bethenabrim 26

Desertum Bethsa ida

Mage dan. 86

Amatha. 8

Aquæ calidæ

Lacus. 64

15.63

44

Dalmanutha 66

Gerasa que et Ger gesa. 55

Hippos. 59

Ephron. 48

55

102

Mare Galilææ.

Bethsaida

Tiberias. o. Cenereth

PATMOS

Listening for God in Rocky Places

For George Washington, Valley Forge tested his faith in the American cause. Sacagawea was sold as a slave but eventually helped Lewis and Clark on their great expedition. Eleanor Roosevelt grew up an insecure, unloved girl, but she became an outspoken human

Name: "My Killing"
Location: 35 miles off Asia Minor coast, p.12
Identification: Rocky island used by the Romans as a penal colony
Story Line: Here the apostle John was exiled and wrote the Revelation
Read it in the Bible: Revelation 1:1–20

rights leader. Thomas Edison had only three months of formal schooling, but his mother encouraged his curiosity and that let to hundreds of useful inventions.

Sometimes what appears to be a detriment to you turns out for your good. That was true of Joseph in the Old Testament (Genesis 50:20) and John in the New Testament (Revelation 1:9).

When the apostle John was banished to a small rocky island off the coast of Asia Minor, he never dreamed how God would use him there. Patmos rises out of the Aegean Sea about thirty–five miles west of Miletus. The island is only ten miles long and six miles wide at its widest point. As an isolated, volcanic island, the Roman historian Tacitus informs us that it was perfect for the Romans to use as a penal colony (*Annals 3.68; 4.30; 15.71*).

John was banished here for fearlessly speaking about Jesus. The Romans thought his time on Patmos would silence him; instead, here is where God spoke to Him the loudest. On this rocky prison God revealed to John future events that will come to pass (Revelation 22:6), and John faithfully wrote them down.

Maybe you're not where you want to be today. Perhaps you're sidelined through illness or unemployment. But be sensitive to God's leading through His Word. This may be the time He speaks most loudly to you too.

PERGAMUM

Subverted by the Culture

Does it sometimes feel like the world is infiltrating the Church? Barna Research indicates that a top concern of Christian youth is "to have a comfortable lifestyle." The church at Pergamum certainly knew the feeling.

NAME: "Citadel"
LOCATION: 80 miles N of Ephesus, p.12
IDENTIFICATION: Cultural center only 20 miles from the Mediterranean coast
STORY LINE: Culture and corruption often are close companions
READ IT IN THE BIBLE: Revelation 1:11; 2:12–17

Pergamum, or Pergamos, was located twenty miles inland from the western coast of Asia Minor on a thousand–foot–high cone–shaped hill. This natural position of strength, along with its religious significance as a temple site, made the city the perfect place to hide wealth. Lysimachus, one of Alexander the Great's generals, hid an enormous sum of money here (9,000 talents), which later was used by the local kings to create the beauty of the city.

Pergamum became a world-class cultural center.
King Eumenes II (197–159 B.C.) expanded the library
to 200,000 volumes and constructed the altar of Zeus
on top of a hill where it could be seen for miles.
Pergamum was the worship center for four Greek
gods—Zeus, Athena, Dionysus, and Asclepius.

Unfortunately, Pergamum's pagan culture had a
profound impact on the church there. Even today some
Christians are following the same path of "loose grace"
that the Pergamum Christians did. They accept what
the Bible teaches . . . until it teaches something they do
not want to believe.

Read John's warning to this
church again and don't allow our
"pick-and-choose" culture to
subvert you. Make sure you and
your church keep asking, "What
does the Bible say?" and do not
be subverted by today's culture
as the Pergamum people were.
God doesn't need another
Pergamum church.

PERSIA

Uncertain Future; Certain God

In London during World War II, Hitler's planes bombed the city routinely. In order to safeguard the children, train loads of them were evacuated to the country. When one young boy was asked, "Where are you going?" he replied, "I don't know, but the king knows." Sometimes you just have to trust the King.

NAME: "Pure" or "Splendid"

LOCATION: E of Mesopotamia, p.13

IDENTIFICATION: Called Fars or Persia, in 1935 this area became known as Iran

STORY LINE: Esther entrusts her uncertain future to a certain God

READ IT IN THE BIBLE: Esther 4:1–17

The young Jewish girl Esther knew what it was to trust God when she became the queen of Persia. A very powerful nation in antiquity, Persia lay just east of Mesopotamia, modern Iraq, and conquered many nations, including Israel. The Persians eventually were conquered by Alexander the Great. Today Persia is called Iran.

The story of Esther is set in the time of the Persian king Xerxes, who reigned between Darius and Artaxerxes (Ezra 4:6) in the middle of the fifth century B.C. Xerxes, also known as Ahasuerus, was married to Queen Vashti, but he deposed her. A search was made throughout the kingdom for a replacement and Esther, or Hadassah, was chosen. But she was a Jewess, not a Persian. Would her heritage be threatened by her new position? She didn't know. Everything was up in the air.

When the vindictive Haman hatched a plan to extinguish the Jews of Persia, only Esther was in a position to save them. Her cousin Mordecai suggested, *"Who knows whether you have come to the kingdom for such a time as this?"* (Esther 4:14). Esther saved the Jews exiled in Persia.

Your future may be uncertain, too. As you feel your way through life, facing multiple challenges, remember Esther. Trust your uncertain future to a certain God.

PHILADELPHIA

Overcomers

More than 1.5 million Christians have been murdered by Muslims in southern Sudan since 1984. In Saudi Arabia, Christians can be arrested for practicing their faith in public. Christians have faced persecution ever since Pentecost.

NAME: "Brotherly Love"
LOCATION: 70 miles NE of Ephesus, p.12
IDENTIFICATION: One of the two Seven Churches not to receive a reproach
STORY LINE: The Christians here faithfully endured persecution
READ IT IN THE BIBLE: Revelation 3:7–13

Tucked away in western Asia Minor was Philadelphia, the city of brotherly love. No, not the home of the Phillies and the Eagles, but the original Philadelphia, founded about 140 B.C. by Attalus II whose nickname was "Philadelphus." Set on a fertile plain, the area around Philadelphia was rich with vineyards and excelled in wine production. But in A.D. 17, Philadelphia was severely damaged by a major earthquake. The Roman emperor Tiberius personally granted disaster aid to rebuild it. By the time the apostle John wrote to the church from his exile on Patmos, the city was thriving once again.

Many of the churches of western Asia were menaced by persecution. However, the Philadelphia believers endured the persecution so gracefully and faithfully that the letter to the church there (Revelation 3:7–13) contains not a single word of reproach or warning. Instead, Jesus encouraged these believers with promises about protection and ultimate victory.

Read about those promises in Revelation 3:7–13 and be encouraged yourself if you are feeling the heat of living out your faith in the world. You are not the first who needs to persevere, and you won't be the last whom Jesus will protect. As our Savior said, we should not fear those who, when they kill us, find no more they can do to us (Luke 12:4). The final victory is to the overcomer, not the persecutor.

PHILIPPI

Giving Living

J. L. Kraft was the founder of Kraft Foods. More than one hundred years later, his products still dominate the dairy isle at your supermarket. But did you know that as a Christian, J. L. Kraft gave approximately 25 percent of his enormous income to Christian ministries? He said,

NAME: "City of Philip"

LOCATION: 200 miles N of Athens, p.12

IDENTIFICATION: Macedonian city visited and written to by the apostle Paul

STORY LINE: The Christians at Philippi were generous and friendly

READ IT IN THE BIBLE: Romans 15:25–28; Philippians 4:10–19; Titus 3:14

"The only investment I ever made which has paid constantly increasing dividends, is the money I have given to the Lord."

Among the New Testament churches, perhaps the church at Philippi was most like Kraft. Philippi was just a minor village in Thrace until about 356 B.C. when Philip II of Macedon, the father of Alexander the Great, conquered and rebuilt it, enlarging and fortifying the city, giving it his name ("Philip's City"). Years later Philippi became a major city in Macedonia and a Roman colony. It was situated on the Ignatian Way, the Roman road that linked the Adriatic and Aegean Seas.

On Paul's second missionary journey, he and Silas were imprisoned in Philippi for preaching the Gospel. On his third missionary journey Paul again passed through Philippi.

In his letter to the Philippians Paul mentioned how grateful he was for their financial assistance. Paul did not write so they would send more money, but so they would know the great reward of the cheerful giver.

Have you discovered the joy of "giving living"? If not, identify a ministry and share with it financially, just as the Philippians did. Remember, you make a living by what you get, but you make a life by what you give. Give more and live more!

PHOENICIA

Reading People Rightly

Forget about Christopher Columbus and his three ships. Forget about Leif Erickson. Forget about all the fearless mariners of the world. None of them can compare to the Phoenicians.

NAME: "Land of Palm Trees"
LOCATION: Land N of Israel, pp.13 & 33
IDENTIFICATION: Seafaring peoples who built ships and became world explorers
STORY LINE: Josiah removed the influence of Israel's neighbors
READ IT IN THE BIBLE: 2 Kings 23:1–25

Phoenicia was a group of city–states whose inhabitants once dominated the waters of the eastern Mediterranean Sea. Although Phoenicia occupied only a strip of the Syrian coastal plain not more than four miles wide at the foot of the Lebanon mountains, Phoenician ships ruled the seas. Almost twenty–one centuries before Vasco de Gama rounded the Cape of Good Hope, the Phoenicians undertook a three–year voyage around Africa. "Phoenicia" was also spelled "Phenice" or "Phenicia."

But while the Phoenicians are admired for their exploits on the high seas, they also adversely affected the faith of the Israelites. The major cities of Phoenicia were Sidon and Tyre. The gods of Sidon are listed among the foreign deities that Israel served (Judges 10:6). Second Kings 23 reads like a laundry list of things Israel should never have been involved in and, thanks to King Josiah, got rid of, at least for a generation or two (2 Kings 23).

Often friends and family have a mixed influence on us. Sometimes they have an affirmative effect on us, and at other times, however, their influence can be destructive. Ezekiel 44:23 suggests that God's people are to know *the difference between the holy and the unholy*" and *"to discern between the unclean and the clean."*

Ask God to give you discernment when those around you have a mixed impact on your life. Learn to appreciate the good but jettison the bad.

PUTEOLI

A Stranger Only Once

Fishermen are known to be rugged, sometimes a bit brusque, and always fearless. In the fall of 1991, a fishing crew on the *Andrea Gail* sailed from the harbor at Gloucester, Massachusetts, into the fishing grounds of the North Atlantic. Two weeks later an event took

NAME: "Little Wells"
LOCATION: 110 miles S of Rome, near Naples, p.12
IDENTIFICATION: Seaport north of the Bay of Naples, modern Pozzuoli
STORY LINE: Paul docked here and stayed seven days with believers
READ IT IN THE BIBLE: Acts 28:11–31

place that had never happened before in recorded history—the perfect storm. The entire crew was lost.

You can find people *"who go down to the sea in ships"* (Psalm 107:23) in every country bounded by water. The fishermen of Puteoli were among them. Located on the north side of the Bay of Naples in southern Italy, Puteoli today is called Pozzuoli

(Acts 28:13). When you visit the ruins of Pompeii, take a few minutes and stop by the neighboring docks of Pozzuoli. The smell of fish is strong in the air. Nets are strewn everywhere to dry. Not much has changed since Paul's day.

When the apostle sailed to Rome to appear before Caesar, he finally ended up at Puteoli. There he stayed with Christians for a week before continuing his journey to Rome (Acts 28:13–14). What turned these rough fishermen into the perfect hosts? The love of Christ. There is a bond between brothers and sisters in Christ that defies cultural explanation. C. S. Lewis remarked, "Is any pleasure on earth as great as a circle of Christian friends by a fire?"

The next time a Christian is visiting your town and needs a place to stay or even just needs a friend, be a Puteolian. Demonstrate the love of Christ the way these fishermen of Puteoli did. Both of you will benefit.

QUMRAN

Amazing Discoveries

Do you know Mohammed ed–Dhib? He's right up there with Marco Polo, Lewis and Clark, and Indiana Jones. In 1947 this unknown Bedouin made the most amazing archaeological discovery of the 20th century— the Dead Sea Scrolls.

NAME: "Two Moons"
LOCATION: NW shore of Dead Sea, p.33
IDENTIFICATION: A desert community for ultra–orthodox Jews called Essenes
STORY LINE: The Dead Sea Scrolls strengthened evidence for the Bible
READ IT IN THE BIBLE: 2 Chronicles 27:1–9

Written between 250 B.C. and A.D. 68, the scrolls represent portions of at least 800 documents that were deposited in the caves near Qumran. Among the 100,000 fragments found, portions of every Old Testament book but Esther were represented, including a complete manuscript of the Book of Isaiah in Hebrew.

The caves where the manuscripts were deposited

were adjacent to Khirbet Qumran, perched on a sandy plateau just west of the northern end of the Dead Sea. Although Qumran is not mentioned in the Bible, King Uzziah built towers or fortifications in the wilderness (2 Chronicles 27:4). Perhaps Qumran was one of them. Here a Jewish community thrived from 130 B.C. to A.D. 135. Here the amazing scrolls were copied, likely by a sect known as the Essenes.

Why are Qumran and the Dead Sea Scrolls so important? Because the Hebrew manuscripts from which the Old Testament was translated date to about 1000 A.D. But the Dead Sea Scrolls are approximately a thousand years older, and their texts are almost identical to the text we already had, proving the amazing accuracy of God's Word.

Can you trust your Bible? The Dead Sea Scrolls say you can. Take some time today to read the Scriptures. It's the most amazing discovery of all. The Bible—read it for answers; read it for life.

RED SEA
Do You Believe in Miracles?

Some people have difficulty believing the miracles in the Bible. They especially have difficulty accepting how Moses parted the Red Sea.

The Red Sea is an arm of the Indian Ocean, nestled between Africa and Asia. About 1,350 miles long, the

NAME: "Sea of Reeds"
LOCATION: Between Egypt and Arabia, p.13
IDENTIFICATION: Arm of the Indian Ocean extending to the northwest
STORY LINE: The Israelites crossed the Red Sea during the Exodus
READ IT IN THE BIBLE: Exodus 13:17–15:22

water is flanked by the Arabian Peninsula on the east and Egypt, the Sudan, Eritrea, and Ethiopia on the west. The Sinai Peninsula splits the northern end of the sea. Here the Gulf of Suez forms the left branch and the Gulf of Aqaba the right.

In Hebrew the "Red" Sea is actually the "reed" sea. Critics often say that if it was a sea of reeds it must have been quite shallow, and therefore there's nothing miraculous about crossing a shallow body of water. But that misses the point. Israel crossed on dry land, shallow or not. Getting a hoard of Israelites completely dry across this sea was no ordinary event.

A teacher attempting to discredit the miracles of the Bible said, "We know the Red Sea was just a marshy area. The water was only six inches deep." A boy in the back of the room shouted, "Praise God for the miracle." Annoyed, the teacher asked, "What miracle?" The boy replied, "The Lord drowned the whole Egyptian army in just six inches of water."

Given enough time and enough minds to think about them, every objection to the authenticity of the Bible proves inadequate. The Bible is not only believable, it is the only book that claims to be infallible. What you don't understand, take by faith. We do this in life every day, why not do the same for the Bible?

RHODES

Sheer Determination

Wilma Rudolph suffered from polio as a child. She wore braces on her legs for over six years. Still, Wilma would not quit. In 1956 she won the bronze medal in the Melbourne Olympics, and four years later she ran for three gold medals in the Rome Olympics.

NAME: "Rose"
LOCATION: 20 miles off Asia Minor coast, p.12
IDENTIFICATION: Island of 500 square miles in the eastern Mediterranean
STORY LINE: Paul is determined to go to Jerusalem as the will of God
READ IT IN THE BIBLE: Acts 21:1–14

The apostle Paul was a man of similar determination. At the end of his third missionary journey he resolved to go to Jerusalem. Paul sailed from Ephesus toward Tyre with stops at Cos, Rhodes, and Patara.

Off the southwest coast of modern Turkey, the beautiful island of Rhodes was an important center for Greek culture. The amazing Colossus of Rhodes straddled the entrance to the island's harbor. At 121 feet tall, the Colossus was roughly the height of the Statue of Liberty. Considered one of the "Seven Wonders of the Ancient World," in 224 B.C. an earthquake broke the statue off at the knees. When Paul docked there he would only have seen the broken remains.

But Paul wouldn't have stayed in Rhodes even if the Colossus had been standing. His face was set toward Jerusalem. Even when Agabus visited Paul in Caesarea and prophesied that he would be captured, Paul reminded everyone that he was not only ready to be jailed for the cause of Christ, he was willing to die for it too (Acts 21:13).

What has God been revealing of His will to you lately? When you are convinced it is truly God's will, don't let anyone dissuade you. Ask God to make His will clear and then never give up.

"*Where is the way to the dwelling of light? And darkness, where is its place?*"

JOB 38:19

ROME

"When in Rome . . ."

Think of Rome and you'll probably think of espresso, pizza, or *Arrivederci Roma*. But what about blood? Once Rome ran red with the blood of the martyrs.

According to legend, Rome was founded in 753 B.C. by twin brothers Romulus and Remus on seven hills

NAME: "Strength"
LOCATION: West central Italy, p.12
IDENTIFICATION: Founded in 753 B.C, Rome became the capital of an empire
STORY LINE: Rome ran red with "the blood of the martyrs"
READ IT IN THE BIBLE: Romans 1:1–17; Acts 28:14–31

some fifteen miles from the mouth of the Tiber River. This was just a dozen years or so before Isaiah had his vision of God (Isaiah 6:1). Although Rome is not mentioned in the Old Testament, the New Testament refers to the city in nine places (Acts 2:10, 18:2, 19:21, 23:11, 28:14, 16, Romans 1:7, 15; and 2 Timothy 1:17). The Caesars ruled during Jesus' lifetime and the

about one thousand yards wide deep in the mountains of western Edom. The only land access to this valley is through a narrow gorge called the Siq. Massive sandstone cliffs rise on both sides, making the Siq or gorge only fifteen feet wide at times. When you visit Petra today you can ride a horse down through the Siq and see the ruins of temples, houses, tombs, and other structures hewn out of the reddish sandstone.

Some Bible scholars believe Petra will one day flourish again as the isolated place in the wilderness promised by God where He would preserve the persecuted Jews during the Great Tribulation (Revelation 12:6). Petra fits this description and has sufficient room to hide thousands of God's people to protect them from Satan's wrath.

Whether or not Petra is the site, we can be certain of one thing: God is our great hiding place. *"You are my hiding place; You shall preserve me from trouble"* (Psalm 32:7). Whatever you need to take shelter from today, let Him be your hiding place.

SHARON

It's a Matter of Time

On a visit to London I took a boat down the Thames
River to Greenwich, England, where the Royal
Observatory determines every time zone in the world
based on "Greenwich mean time" or "Greenwich
meridian time." It is an impressive place, even by

NAME: "Plain"
LOCATION: Western Israel, p.33
IDENTIFICATION: Israel's coastal plain stretching south from
    Mount Carmel
STORY LINE: God will blossom the wilderness as the Rose of Sharon
READ IT IN THE BIBLE: Song of Solomon 2:1; Isaiah 35:1–10

British standards. Today, however, the new cesium
atomic clock (NIST–F1) is more far accurate than the
huge timepieces of Greenwich. The NIST–F1 will not
vary by a single second in nearly 20 million years.
That's pretty amazing, but it's inconsequential
compared to the accuracy of God's timetable.

God does everything according to His own timing.

For example, Isaiah predicted that one day the *"desert shall rejoice and blossom as the rose . . . The excellence of Carmel and Sharon"* (Isaiah 35:1–2).

Sharon is the largest coastal plain of Israel, stretching nearly fifty miles from Mount Carmel to the suburbs of Tel Aviv. Approximately ten miles wide, in biblical times this lowland region was renowned for its beauty and fertility (1 Chronicles 27:29). The Via Maris, a major north–south trading route, hugged the eastern edge of the plain. Five streams or wadis cross the Sharon Plain.

God promised that one day even the deserts of the Holy Land would blossom like a rose; they would resemble the fertile plain of Sharon. If God can make the desert sands blossom, imagine what He can do with your life. It's only a matter of time. If you're not satisfied with things as they are, take heart and remember that God makes everything beautiful in its time (Ecclesiastes 3:11). Set your life to God's timetable and watch Him work.

SILOAM

It's All About Obedience

One of life's hardest lessons is that just as disobedience brings heartache and failure, obedience brings happiness and blessing. Perhaps you've already experienced this in your own life. The man born blind whose story is recorded in John 9 certainly had.

NAME: "Sent"

LOCATION: Immediately S of Jerusalem, p.53

IDENTIFICATION: Jerusalem water supply at the opening to Hezekiah's Tunnel

STORY LINE: Jesus healed a blind man who washed his eyes in this pool

READ IT IN THE BIBLE: John 9:1–25

Jesus and the Twelve were leaving the temple when they encountered a blind man. While the disciples wanted to assign blame for the man's blindness, Jesus wanted to help the man. The Savior spat on the ground, formed a clay salve, and spread it on the man's eyes. Jesus then sent him to the pool of Siloam to wash his eyes.

The pool of Siloam was the outlet for Hezekiah's tunnel, dug during the threat of the Assyrian invasion about 700 B.C. (2 Kings 20:20; 2 Chronicles 32:2–4). The tunnel brought water from the Gihon Spring, Jerusalem's only natural source of water, a third of a mile through the subterranean rock under the city wall to the Pool of Siloam. Today the fifty–foot by five–foot pool lies outside the Old City of Jerusalem.

The issue in this story was not medicine. The issue was faith. There was no medicinal benefit to the combination of Jesus' spittle and temple dust. You won't find this as a cure for blindness in any medical encyclopedia. The real issue was, would the man obey, even if he didn't understand?

That's the issue with us too. When we obey the Lord, even if we don't understand His command, the result is always God's blessing. If you want a blessing like the man born blind, follow the advice of Jesus' mother: *"Whatever He says to you, do it"* (John 2:5).

MOUNT SINAI

Something Better for You

Of all the great contrasts in life—red states and blue states, men from Mars and women from Venus—the greatest is the contrast between law and grace. The Mosaic Law is symbolized by Mount Sinai. God's grace is exemplified by Mount Calvary.

NAME: "Thorny"

LOCATION: Western Arabia, p.13

IDENTIFICATION: The Mountain of God where Moses received the Decalogue

STORY LINE: Mount Sinai represents the Old Covenant, life under the Law

READ IT IN THE BIBLE: Exodus 19:1–20; Galatians 4:21–26

Mount Sinai is where God met Moses and gave him the Ten Commandments and the rest of the Law. Sinai defines not only the mountain, but the desert around it (Leviticus 7:38), the entire peninsula incorporated by the Gulf of Suez on the west, and the Gulf of Aqaba on the east.

The traditional location of Mount Sinai is at the

southern end of the Sinai Peninsula. The Greek Orthodox monastery of Saint Catherine was constructed between 527 and 565 A.D. at the base of the 7,500–foot peak of Jebel Musa (Mount Moses in Arabic). Recently some scholars have suggested that the traditional site is wrong and the real Mount Sinai is across the Gulf of Aqaba in ancient Midian or Arabia (Exodus 3:1; Galatians 4:25).

Most references to Mount Sinai are found in Exodus, Leviticus, and Numbers, but in Galatians 4:21–26 the apostle Paul gives new meaning to the old mountain when he suggests that Mount Sinai represents the old covenant, the Law, and spiritual slavery. The new covenant, by contrast, presents better things (Hebrews 6:9; 7:17–22)—a better promise, plans, country, sacrifice, and the like—and is provided through the blood of Jesus.

Today we no longer bow to the Law of Sinai; we bow to the Lord of Calvary.

SMYRNA

Poor, But Rich

Some people can't understand why, if God loves poor people, He doesn't make them rich. The problem is that although we equate wealth with blessing, God doesn't.

For example, years ago I attended church with a remarkable family who had a passel of kids and hardly

NAME: "Myrrh"
LOCATION: 30 miles NW of Ephesus, p.12
IDENTIFICATION: Modern Izmir, Turkey, one of Revelation's Seven Churches
STORY LINE: Not all wealth is found in a financial portfolio
READ IT IN THE BIBLE: Revelation 2:8–11

two nickels to rub together. They always seemed to be running themselves ragged, but they were clean, cheerful, and incessant workers with the children's program in our church. Everybody loved and respected them.

The church at Smyrna was filled with people like that. The early residents of Smyrna recognized the dominance of Pergamum and transferred their allegiance to Rome, the rising superpower at the time. In 195 B.C. Smyrna, which today is called Izmir, Turkey, built a temple dedicated to the worship of the Roman emperor. As a result, the city prospered under Roman rule.

With the influence of emperor worship so strong in Smyrna, many Christians found it difficult to keep good jobs; consequently they were poor. Still, as one of the Seven Churches of Revelation, Jesus commended them. He told them He knew all about their poverty, and He promised that if they would be faithful to Him, He would give them the crown of life (Revelation 2:10).

Being poor in this world's goods does not mean you are poor in what really matters. Sometimes wealth becomes an obstacle to service. If it does, you are better off poor now with the promise of eternal blessing than being rich now and robbed of eternal blessing. *For what will it profit a man if he gains the whole world, and loses his own soul?"* (Mark 8:36).

Choose carefully what you consider real wealth. You may get your wish.

SODOM

If You Linger, You Lose

Some things just seem to go together, like salt and pepper, Abbott and Costello, or peanut butter and jelly.

Sodom and Gomorrah are like that. Although Sodom became prominent, the pair were actually part

NAME: "Place of Lime"
LOCATION: Southern end of Dead Sea, p.33
IDENTIFICATION: One of the five cities of the Valley of Siddim (i.e. Salt Sea)
STORY LINE: Sodom is synonymous with sexual perversity and divine judgment
READ IT IN THE BIBLE: Genesis 19:1–29

of five cities located in the Valley of Siddim at the southern end of the Dead Sea. Mentioned thirty–six times in Genesis, Sodom became the supreme example of a city enamored with sexual deviance.

Sodom's destruction (Genesis 19) was used as a warning of God's judgment on other sinful people and places (Deuteronomy 29:23; Isaiah 1:9–10; Jeremiah 23:14; Jeremiah 49:18; Lamentations 4:6; Amos 4:11;

Zephaniah 2:9). So powerful was God's hatred for the sins of Sodom that the city's destruction even found its way onto the pages of the New Testament (Matthew 10:15; Luke 10:12; 17:29; Romans 9:29; 2 Peter 2:6; Jude 7; Revelation 11:8).

When Abraham's nephew moved to Sodom, the godly Abraham knew it was a mistake. The men of Sodom had ravenous sexual appetites and would stop at nothing to gratify them. God warned Lot to leave Sodom before it was destroyed. Yet, remarkably, Lot lingered, not wanting to separate himself from Sodom's sin.

Often we do that. We know what we are doing displeases God, but we are reluctant to leave it behind. We want the pleasure of our sin. But real pleasure comes in confessing and forsaking sin, not in hanging on to it. Don't linger when God tells you to give it up. Forgiveness is always better than fire and brimstone.

SPAIN

'To Spain and Beyond'

If Buzz Lightyear had lived during New Testament times, his famous "to infinity and beyond" might have become "to Spain and beyond." Spain is the most westerly peninsula in southwestern Europe and was considered by most Romans to be the western limit of their empire.

NAME: "Scarceness"
LOCATION: Western European peninsula, p.12
IDENTIFICATION: The most westerly part of the known world in Paul's day
STORY LINE: Paul's plan for world evangelism included reaching Spain
READ IT IN THE BIBLE: Romans 15:22–33

The Phoenicians extended their commercial empire to the Iberian Peninsula as early as 1100 B.C. From the center of their empire at Carthage, they launched a series of colonial expeditions to Spain, establishing settlements at Carthage Nova (now Cartagena), Malacca (now Malaga), and Tartessus (where Jonah attempted to flee from God). The Romans expelled the

The original name of the city was Shechem, which in Hebrew meant "slope" or "shoulder," but the Greek form of that Hebrew name is Sychar, which means "drunken." Here Jacob dug a well, the water from which is still cold and refreshing today.

When Jesus arrived at that well, a woman from the village came to draw water. Jesus asked her for a drink. When she hesitated the Savior told her He could give her living water (John 4:14). She came to believe in Jesus as Messiah and Savior, and so did many of the villagers.

Jesus never hesitated to introduce eternity into His ordinary conversations, and neither should we. After all, the people we casually encounter are as much in need of a Savior as those to whom we specifically plan to witness. Let the fact that you have been satisfied by God's living water be a frequent part of your conversations.

SYRIA

Leaving a Legacy

What will your legacy be? Will you leave behind
something of value to others? Maybe thinking about
Syria will stimulate your thoughts about a lasting legacy.

Syria was called Aram in the Bible. The Arameans
originated in upper Mesopotamia early in the second

NAME: "Exalted"
LOCATION: Land NE of Israel, pp.13 & 33
IDENTIFICATION: Land of the Aramean tribes which included the
city Haran
STORY LINE: Aramaic, the language Jesus used, is preserved today
READ IT IN THE BIBLE: Mark 5:21–43; 1 Corinthians 16:22

millennium B.C. Bethuel and Laban were both
Arameans (Genesis 25:20; Genesis 28:1–7). Hosea
recalls that Jacob fled to *"the field of Aram"* (Hosea
12:12) or *"Aram–naharaim"* (Aram of the two rivers—
Tigris and Euphrates). By about 1100 B.C., the
Arameans spread west and moved into the territory
near the Jordan River. That's when they came into

conflict with Israel. King David defeated Hadadezer, king of Aram–zobah (2 Samuel 8:3–4). Ahab, Ahaziah, Jehoram, Jehu, Jehoahaz, and Jehoash all had conflicts with Damascus, Syria's capital. When Assyria to the north and east collapsed in 612–609 B.C., the whole region came under Babylonian, then Persian, then Greek, and finally Roman control.

Although Syria's power has diminished over the centuries, the people of Aram gave the world something better than power. They gave us their language. Aramaic was the language Jesus spoke. Several Aramaic words like *"talitha cumi"* (Mark 5:41) and *"marana tha"* (1 Corinthians 16:22 NASB) have found their way into the Bible. The Christian form of Aramaic, Syriac, has left behind a huge legacy of literature—histories, theologies, commentaries, and translations.

What will your legacy be? Live wisely because today you are building your legacy. Make sure it's both a valuable one and a long–lasting one.

261

MOUNT TABOR

Only Jesus

Everybody needs friends, especially close friends. Seventy people made up the core of Jesus' followers, but He had only twelve apostles. And only three of them were part of His inner circle.

NAME: "Height"
LOCATION: 61 miles N of Jerusalem, p.33
IDENTIFICATION: Mountain in the Jezreel Valley that rises sharply to 1900 feet
STORY LINE: Jesus was transfigured before Peter, James and John
READ IT IN THE BIBLE: Matthew 17:1–13

One day Jesus took His closest friends—Peter, James, and John—with Him to the top of a mountain, likely Mount Tabor. Rising steeply as a round mound 1,900 feet above sea level, Tabor is at the eastern end of the Jezreel Valley, about six miles from Nazareth. Here Deborah and Barak fought against Sisera (Judges 4:1–24), and Gideon confronted the Midianite kings Zebah and Zalmunna here after they had killed his brothers (Judges 8:18).

Since the fourth century, Mount Tabor has been identified as the possible site of Jesus' Transfiguration. Helena, the mother of Emperor Constantine, was so convinced the Transfiguration occurred here that in A.D. 326 she built a church on the top. Today a monastery and a basilica crown the mountain.

When Jesus was transfigured, His friends saw Moses and Elijah on the mountain with Him. Peter suggested they erect three shrines, one for each, but God gave the audible reply, *"This is My beloved Son, in whom I am well pleased. Hear Him!"* The disciples fell on their faces in fear, and when they looked up again, *"They saw no one but Jesus only"* (Matthew 17:5–8).

Moses and Elijah are great. Your pastor, teacher, or favorite musician may be gifted. But only Jesus is the Savior and Messiah. Today, see no one but Jesus for your salvation, your source, your strength. There's no one like Jesus.

TARSHISH

Far From God

Years ago the village priest in Kalinovaka, Russia, took a special interest in a boy who recited his Scriptures with piety. The boy even learned to quote the four gospels, which he recited nonstop in church one day. But sixty years later the priest's prize pupil, Nikita Khrushchev,

NAME: "Yellow Jasper"
LOCATION: Land distant from Israel, p.12
IDENTIFICATION: Tarshish was a trading partner with many Middle East nations
STORY LINE: Tarshish was synonymous with being distant from God
READ IT IN THE BIBLE: Ezekiel 27:1–28:19

was far from God when became the premier of the Soviet Union.

When the writers of the Bible wanted to depict a place far from God, they chose Tarshish. No one knows exactly where Tarshish was, but most scholars believe it was a seaport on the coast of Spain, where the name Tartessus hints at Tarshish. The place is mentioned about two dozen times in the Bible, usually in relationship with commerce and ships (Psalm 48:7; Isaiah 2:14). Solomon sent his ships to trade with Tarshish (2 Chronicles 9:21). So did Jehoshaphat (2 Chronicles 20:36–37). And several prophecies condemned Tarshish for aligning itself with Tyre (Isaiah 23; Ezekiel 27–28).

But more than anything, Tarshish meant being far from Israel and far from Israel's God (Isaiah 60:9; 66:19). When the prophet Jonah attempted to flee from the presence of the Lord, he went to Joppa and purchased a ticket to Tarshish (Jonah 1:3).

People still try to distance themselves from God. Maybe you're one of them. Tarshish has become your destination, but God offers you something better. He offers you a home. Jesus said, *"In my Father's house are many mansions"* (John 14:2). Stop running and start trusting.

TARSUS

Forever Changed

Clyde Thompson was "the meanest man in Texas." He first killed two men in 1928 at the age of 17, and for the crime he was sent to prison. While on death row he killed four inmates. Clyde was so fierce that the warden locked him up in an unused prison morgue and

NAME: "A Flat Basket"
LOCATION: Eastern Asia Minor, p.13
IDENTIFICATION: Tarsus was the capital of the Roman province of Cilicia
STORY LINE: Saul of Tarsus became the apostle Paul by God's grace
READ IT IN THE BIBLE: Acts 9:1–25

welded the door shut. But someone gave Clyde a Bible, and he began to read it. His life was dramatically changed. After the governor pardoned him, Clyde Thompson began telling everyone he encountered how Christ could change their lives, too.

Saul of Tarsus had a similar story. Tarsus was the capital of the Roman province Cilicia in Asia Minor.

It was a university town on the Cydnus River, twelve miles upstream from the Mediterranean Sea. It was also famous as a tent–making center. Out of this town came a young Jew bound for Jerusalem to study under the famous Gamaliel.

After intense rabbinical training and the violent start of a promising career, something happened to Saul on the road from Jerusalem to Damascus. The incident is recorded in Acts 9. He was blinded by a bright light and heard a voice that asked, *"Saul, Saul, why are you persecuting Me?"* He knew it was the Lord. Trembling and astonished, Saul trusted Jesus Christ as his Savior, and his life was demonstrably changed. He became the apostle Paul. Like Clyde Thompson, the change was radical and it was deep.

Although not always as perceptible, that's the kind of change that comes to everyone who expresses faith in Christ as Savior. It's the kind of change that makes your present enjoyable and your future secure.

THESSALONICA

Guilt By Association

If you and your family take a vacation to Las Vegas, does that mean you are going there to gamble? If you are a Democrat, are you also a liberal? If you attended Notre Dame, are you a Catholic?

NAME: "Victory of Falsity"
LOCATION: 200 miles N of Athens, p.12
IDENTIFICATION: Chief city of Macedonia and center of Roman government
STORY LINE: Persecution of Christians is as old as the church itself
READ IT IN THE BIBLE: Acts 17:1–9

Our associations do not always make us guilty, but they often identify our preferences. When Paul carried the Gospel into Europe, his second stop was Thessalonica, the chief city of Macedonia, the northern part of Greece. As the Roman administrative center of the region, it had both an excellent harbor and was located on the Egnatian Way, the major overland route east from Italy.

When Paul arrived at the city he immediately went into the synagogue and reasoned with those present about Jesus being the Messiah and Savior. While only a few Jews believed, a great crowd of God–fearing Greeks and some of the leading women of the city came to faith in Christ. The success of Paul's preaching aroused the jealousy of the local Jewish leaders. Instead of confronting Paul or debating him, they simply paid some thugs from the marketplace to storm the house of Jason where Paul was a guest. Paul wasn't there so they dragged Jason from his own house and accused him of being guilty by association with those *"who have turned the world upside down"* (Acts 17:6).

If you are known around town or at work as a caring Christian, don't be embarrassed. Let your friends know of your faith. That's the kind of association to plead guilty to.

THREE INNS

Encouragement

A London newspaper once challenged Harry Houdini to escape from a special pair of handcuffs. On March 17, 1904, while four thousand people looked on at the London Hippodrome, a manacled Houdini disappeared into an empty cabinet. Twenty minutes later he stood up.

NAME: "Three Taverns"
LOCATION: 33 miles S of Rome, p.12
IDENTIFICATION: Village at Appian Way junction, a traveler's meeting place
STORY LINE: Believers encouraged Paul here on his journey to Rome
READ IT IN THE BIBLE: Acts 28:1–16

Thinking he was free, the crowd cheered. But Houdini disappeared back into the cabinet. Thirty minutes later he stood up again to loud applause, but still he wasn't free! Finally, Houdini leaped from the cabinet waving the handcuffs over his head. Later, he confessed that he stood up both times because he needed encouragement to keep him going.

We're all like that. Occasionally just a word of encouragement keeps us going. After being shipwrecked on the way to Rome, Paul needed some encouragement. It had been a long, arduous journey. Besides, he was on his way to Rome to stand trial.

When he arrived at Puteoli, he made his way north toward Rome. At a place called Three Inns or Three Taverns, some Christians gathered to encourage him. This village was just a wide spot on the Appian Way at milepost 33, near modern Cisterna, but it was a huge boost for the weary apostle. Seeing those Christians buoyed Paul's spirits as much as when a runner nearing the finish line hears the cheering crowd (Acts 28:15).

Does someone need you to bolster them today? A little bit of encouragement goes a long way.

THYATIRA

Making the Last, the Best

Michelangelo was appointed architect of St. Peter's Cathedral in Rome at age 71. He held that office until his death at age 89. He overcame some early difficulties and disputes to allow his genius and skill to reach its peak at the end of his life.

NAME: "Odor of Affliction"
LOCATION: 75 miles NE of Ephesus, p.12
IDENTIFICATION: One of Seven Churches of Revelation in a strategic location
STORY LINE: The church's best works were her last works
READ IT IN THE BIBLE: Revelation 2:18–29

So it was with the church at Thyatira, the smallest of the seven churches mentioned in Revelation. Located forty miles southeast of Pergamos, the small town of Thyatira was a commercial center known for the dyeing industry. The people manufactured an expensive purple dye made from the madder root and a shellfish called morex. Lydia, the first known Christian in Europe, was a businesswoman from Thyatira (Acts 16:14–15, 40) who traded in the costly purple garments exported from there. She opened her home to Paul, and her whole household was saved with her.

God had something commendable to say to all but two of the seven churches of Revelation. For the church at Thyatira, He noted that they possessed love, service, faith, and patience. Moreover, He commended them that their last works were more than their first. Yes, there was criticism for the church—mainly that they followed a spiritual Jezebel into carnality—but the believers of Thyatira recovered from their misbehavior and became overcomers. They didn't permit their sin to destroy them.

Let's face it. You're going to have ups and downs in your life. What's important is that you come to grips with your sin, repent of it, and learn from it. Do that and your last works will be your best works.

UR of the CHALDEES

Armed With Nothing But Faith

Faith doesn't mean believing despite an absence of facts; it's believing despite an absence of sight.

Born in Ur of the Chaldees, Abraham is a great example of faith in God's Word. Although mentioned

---

NAME: "Flame of the Clod–breakers"

LOCATION: Lower Mesopotamia, p.13

IDENTIFICATION: Center for the worship of Nannar or Sin, the moon god

STORY LINE: Abraham left his homeland out of faith in God

READ IT IN THE BIBLE: Genesis 11:28–12:5

---

only four times in the Bible (Genesis 11:28, 31; 15:7; Nehemiah 9:7), the existence of Ur is not in doubt. Archaeologists have unearthed large portions of this site and have found clay tablets telling of life in the city. We know that schools there instructed students in writing cuneiform, multiplication, division, and even figuring square and cube roots. Ur's houses often had two stories with as many as twenty rooms. Many art objects made of precious metals and other costly materials have been excavated. To say the least, Abraham's hometown was a sophisticated place.

But when God called Abraham to leave the familiarity of Ur and go to a yet undisclosed place, Abraham never hesitated. Not because he could see the future, but because he could trust God. In a city known for other gods, Abraham knew one true God of the universe. Abraham trusted God's character, not what he could see ahead.

That's the way it must be with you and me. We trust our unknown future to a God we know. Concentrate on knowing God better and you will not be driven by faith in what lies *ahead* of you or by faith in what lies *within* you, but by faith in the God who *stands behind* you.

UZ

Our Greatest Asset

The story of Job is more about integrity than about patience or how to handle great loss. Job had a commitment to righteousness that superceded everything else he had in life.

NAME: "Counsel" or "Firmness"
LOCATION: Arabia, E of Edom, pp.13 & 33
IDENTIFICATION: Desert land populated by descendants of the Horites of Seir
STORY LINE: Wealthy Job feared God and shunned evil, even in disaster
READ IT IN THE BIBLE: Job 1:1–22

The Book of Job begins with the familiar phrase, *"There was a man in the land of Uz, whose name was Job; and that man was blameless and upright, and one who feared God and shunned evil"* (Job 1:1). That pretty much sums up Job's story. The book does not actually give the location of Uz, only that it was in the East (Job 1:3). It also says Job's attackers were Sabeans (1:15) and Chaldeans (1:17), desert peoples. The land of Uz appears to be somewhere east of the land of Israel, probably east of Edom in northern Arabia.

Where Uz was doesn't matter nearly as much as who Job was. He was an extremely wealthy sheik with a large family and vast animal resources. To say that he was the greatest of all the people of the East is not hyperbole. But what made Job truly great was his piety, not his prosperity. Job was the real deal. He knew that fearing God was the essence of wisdom (Proverbs 1:7) and that anyone who fears God lives accordingly. So he both shunned evil and lived blamelessly before God and a watching world.

Your greatest asset is not your portfolio but your integrity. If you want to please God, learn to reverence Him by both what you say and how you live. Live to be blameless, so that no charge made against you will stick.

VIA DOLOROSA

The Street Jesus Took

Some streets are known for their elaborate lighting displays at Christmastime, like the Champs Elysee in Paris. Others are known for extravagant parades, like Fifth Avenue in New York City. But one street is known for its sorrow.

NAME: "Way of Sorrows"
LOCATION: Street in north Jerusalem, p.53
IDENTIFICATION: A famous street in the Old City of Jerusalem
STORY LINE: Jesus carried His cross from the Praetorium to Golgotha
READ IT IN THE BIBLE: Luke 23:1–33

It has been the scene of long processionals of people bearing crosses. It has also been the scene of unrest in the Palestinian intifada. It is the Via Dolorosa, bustling with shops, tourists, and ordinary people making their way from one part of Jerusalem's Old City to another. But on one ancient day it was the scene of supreme humiliation, shame, and sorrow.

Jesus was sentenced to die in the Roman manner—crucifixion. Such executions were done outside the city, so the Savior was forced to carry the patibulum or crossbar of His cross to the place He would die. The route He took was the Via Dolorosa.

Although the Via Dolorosa and most of its traditional fourteen stations of the cross are not mentioned in the Bible, one thing is clear. Jesus walked this way to Calvary, where the innocent One died for the guilty. *For He (God the Father) made Him (God the Son) who knew no sin be sin for us, that we might become the righteousness of God in Him"* (2 Corinthians 5:21).

It's not important that you join a processional walking the Via Dolorosa, but it is important that you have faith in the One who did it alone. Salvation doesn't come through a pilgrimage; it comes through a Savior, and Jesus is the only Savior this world will ever have. Trust Him today. Then thank Him, too.

WATER GATE

Reading Is Fundamental

On September 9, 1971, the White House "plumbers" unit burglarized an office at the Watergate Complex, leading to the downfall of the Nixon presidency.

But the bungling burglars were not history's most important Water Gate gathering. Of the ten gates

> NAME: "Water Gate"
> LOCATION: East side of Jerusalem, p.53
> IDENTIFICATION: One of the principal gates on the east side of Jerusalem
> STORY LINE: Here the people of God assembled when Ezra read the Law
> READ IT IN THE BIBLE: Nehemiah 8:1–18

leading into Jerusalem in Nehemiah's day, one was called the Water Gate. The exact location of this ancient gate is uncertain, but when Nehemiah arrived in Jerusalem to repair the wall, the Water Gate was among those repaired on the eastern side of the city (Nehemiah 3:26). This gate was north of the stairs that ascended from the City of David, the original site of

David's Jerusalem, on the southern edge of modern Jerusalem (Nehemiah 12:37).

The Water Gate was an assembly point for the people. When the builders of Nehemiah's wall faced opposition and needed encouragement, Ezra read the Book of the Law there and then explained it. The practical application was evident: all the people wept when they heard the Law (Nehemiah 8:9).

Every time you read your Bible you should ask three questions:

What does the Bible say?
What does it mean?
What does it mean to me?

If you ask these three questions each time you read God's Word, it will open your understanding of the Bible like it did for the people at the Water Gate.

YARMUK

The Wrong Side of the Tracks

Jesus was both a man of God and a man of the people. Being from an out–of–the–way place like Nazareth did not give Him much of a power base, but what He did for the common people—teaching them, healing them, encouraging them—endeared Jesus to many.

NAME: "Mercy"
LOCATION: E of Jordan River, p.33
IDENTIFICATION: A river close to the southern end of the Sea of Galilee
STORY LINE: Jesus was popular among the cities near the Yarmuk River
READ IT IN THE BIBLE: Matthew 4:13–25

Most of Jesus' ministry took place on and around the Sea of Galilee. He usually was found along the northern and western shores of the Galilee, but He also had a huge following among those living on the other side of the sea, which was tantamount to living "on the other side of the tracks."

A major water source in this area—east of the

Jordan River and close to the southern end of the Sea of Galilee—was the Yarmuk River. Although not mentioned by name in the Bible, the Yarmuk was an important source of water. Not far from the Yarmuk were many of the cities of the Decapolis. Matthew 4:25 indicates that great crowds (mostly Greeks and Canaanites) followed Jesus during His early ministry in the area around the Yarmuk. And the story of the demoniac whom Jesus healed and who immediately began to tell people what Jesus had done for him (Mark 5:20), occurred near here.

If you could see the Yarmuk today you'd think it wasn't much of a river. But maybe that's why Jesus was loved by so many of the people in this area. Jesus didn't go looking for the high or mighty but for the insignificant and needy. Maybe that's good news for you and me today. We can be from the wrong side of the tracks and still be on the right train.

ZION

City of Our God

John Newton (1725–1807) is best remembered as the slave–trader–turned–preacher who wrote "Amazing Grace." But Newton also wrote many other hymns while he pastored the church in Olney, England. One of them begins with the words, "Glorious things of Thee are spoken, Zion, city of our God."

NAME: "Fortification"
LOCATION: SE edge of Jerusalem, p.53
IDENTIFICATION: Mountainside fortress of Jerusalem first taken by David
STORY LINE: When you go to Zion, you go to be in the presence of God
READ IT IN THE BIBLE: 1 Chronicles 11:1–9; Psalm 84

The first occurrence in the Bible of the word "Zion" is in the story of David's conquest of Jerusalem (2 Samuel 5:6–10). David captured the Jebusite "stronghold of Zion" which became known as the "City of David." This stronghold refers to an eleven–acre site on the southeastern ridge of the mountain on which

Solomon would later build his temple. Once the city expanded north to include the temple area, the entire city became affectionately known as Zion.

Because Zion is the city of God, pilgrims trekked up the mountains to Jerusalem. The pilgrim songs (Psalms 84, 122, 125–128) demonstrate the deep longing of these people to be in God's presence. That should be our desire, too.

Being with Him was also John Newton's desire and the reason he wrote about "Zion, city of our God." The hymn was set to a tune written by Franz Joseph Haydn, who once wrote, "When I think of the divine Being, my heart is so full of joy that the notes fly off as from a spindle, and as I have a cheerful heart, He will pardon me if I serve Him cheerfully."

Joyful service to God arises from a deep longing for God. Take some time today to read Psalm 84. Make your own pilgrimage to Zion, to the heart of God.

ZOAR

Right Motives; Wrong Actions

American church leader Bob Jones, Sr., used to say, "It's never right to do wrong to do right." That's something we all need to learn. So did Lot's daughters.

When the angels told Lot to get out of Sodom because God was about to destroy the five cities of the

NAME: "Little"
LOCATION: Southern end of Dead Sea, p.33
IDENTIFICATION: One of the city-states of the plain where Lot chose to live
STORY LINE: Here Lot was duped into fathering children by his daughters
READ IT IN THE BIBLE: Genesis 19:1–38

plain, Lot reluctantly left Sodom but only went to Zoar, one of the other cities of the plain. Zoar was located near the southeast corner of the Dead Sea (Genesis 13:10). When Moses surveyed the Promised Land from Mount Pisgah, Zoar was positioned as the southern terminus of the plain of the Jericho Valley (Deuteronomy 34:3).

Lot believed that because Zoar was just a little town, God wouldn't destroy it. But Lot repeatedly had shown a penchant for not fully obeying God, and his daughters obviously acquired that trait, too. After their mother was turned to salt for her own disobedience (Genesis 19:26), the daughters observed that there were no men readily available to father children by them. So they did something wrong in order to carry on the family line. They got their father drunk and used Lot to impregnate them. From these unholy unions came the Ammonites from one daughter and the Moabites from the other. These nations descended from Lot's daughters would be two of Israel's fiercest, longtime enemies (Genesis 19:36–38).

When you're faced with a problem that appears to be easily solved if you only do one thing wrong, think again. Two wrongs don't make a right; neither does a single wrong ever make things right. Ask God to help you do the right thing every time.

For More Information

Dr. Woodrow Kroll is president and senior Bible teacher for the international media ministry Back to the Bible. The *Back to the Bible* radio broadcast—in twenty–five languages—can be heard by more than 50 percent of the world's population every day. Dr. Kroll is the author of more than three dozen books, including *People in the Bible.* His clear, incisive teaching of the Word keeps him in demand as a speaker all over the world. Says Woodrow Kroll, "My greatest joy is preaching the Word of God." He and his wife, Linda, reside in Ashland, Nebraska, near the international headquarters of Back to the Bible.

Here's how you can reach Back to the Bible:
www.backtothebible.org
Back to the Bible
P.O. Box 82808
Lincoln, NE 67501
info@backtothebible.com | 402–464–7200